GLORIOUS PATCHWORK

GLORIOUS PATCHWORK
MORE THAN 25 GLORIOUS QUILT DESIGNS

KAFFE FASSETT

with Liza Prior Lucy

Special photography by Debbie Patterson

Little, Brown and Company (Canada) Limited

BOSTON • NEW YORK • TORONTO • LONDON

First published 1997

1 3 5 7 9 10 8 6 4 2

Editor: Sally Harding
Art Director: Polly Dawes
Photographer: Debbie Patterson
Patchwork flat shot photography and front cover: Dave King
Picture research: Mary Jane Gibson
Patchwork instruction diagrams: Ethan Danielson
Techniques illustrations: Kate Simuneck

First published in Canada in 1997 by Little, Brown and Company (Canada) Limited
148 Yorkville Avenue, Toronto, ON M5R 1C2

First published in the United Kingdom in 1997 by
Ebury Press Limited
Random House, 20 Vauxhall Bridge Road, London SW1V 2SA

Canadian Cataloguing in Publication Data
Fassett, Kaffe
   Glorious patchwork quilts

ISBN 0-316-27530-1
1. Quilting - Patterns.   I. Title.
TT835.F37 1997   746.9'7   C96-931410-8

Colour reproduction by Masterlith Limited, UK
Printed and bound in Italy by Amilcare Pizzi, Milan

61,262

ontents

Introduction

Sitting down to write puts me in an analytical mood. What is the essence of my helter-skelter life and the many treasured objects that I bring home from my travels? The one thing that most of my collection of pots, fabrics and beadwork possess is a bold or intricate use of pattern, usually in strong colours. As you can see, this feeds into my design work. Over the years pattern has become more and more of an obsession. To me it is one of the magic elements of life that never loses its fascination. I can spend hours painting furniture or covering surfaces with mosaic. How astounding it is to see the plainest square box or cylinder acquire movement and lightness through surface decoration.

On the most basic level, with patchwork one is taking a rectangle or a square and try-ing to inject movement and colour into its broad plane. You can get a strong sense of this piecing-together of pattern when flying over farmland – those huge or tiny fields of various shades unfolding below are an inspiring sight! I frequently find myself trying to emulate the close tones of that landscape of fields by selecting fabrics with very subtle differences and putting them together. Much of the breathtaking work in museums and old houses has faded to a similar close toning. This closeness can be of saturated hues, as in my Zinnia 2-by-2 Quilt (see page 36), or of very delicate ones, as in the Pastel 2-by-2 Quilt (see page 17).

Making arrangements with fragments of existing pattern is a whole world of joy. It never ceases to tickle me how a fragment of boring fabric or mundane crockery can acquire a magic jauntiness when fit together with other patterned fragments to form

ABOVE This display of nails and screws in a market in Vietnam looks like a carpet of jewels. It reminds us what a versatile motif the simple square is.
RIGHT My Striped Venetian Tile Quilt shows the square used as the basis for a design. The geometric structure comes from a thirteenth-century marble tile floor in St Mark's Cathedral in Venice.

glorious patchworks or mosaics – foreign worlds joining to create delicious hybrids. It is not knowing what will happen until we try a certain combination that makes the process so exciting when it works. Not only works, but sparks, making each of the patterns livelier and more handsome in their relating.

Perhaps those of us who love this collid-ing of patterns are hankering after a lusher age when there was more decoration in our everyday lives. When I visit old Norwegian, Spanish or Mexican churches, I experience a childlike delight in all the flourishing paint-ed and carved surfaces. The rich fullness of it satisfies something deep in my soul.

A strong element in the appeal of patch-work is the abstracting of images that might otherwise get too sentimental. When flower prints on pastel grounds are cut at odd

angles and sewn to fruit prints or crash into other fragments of flowers, they take on a whole new excitement that transcends the over-sweet original. Slotting together organic prints and textured colours in arbitrary geometric layouts produces unexpectedly satisfying results. And this geometry can be as simple as a layout of squares. Looking to the rich past of old quilts, I am dazzled by the never-ending inventiveness of arrangements of squares. It makes me search the world for more variations on square designs, like those found in stunning tile floors or even in the arrangement of Vietnamese nail and screw boxes in the Hanoi market (see facing page).

Why patchwork? Those who know about my knitting books most likely know about the spontaneous way that obsession started. How, as a painter working in London, I stumbled on an irresistible collection of coloured yarns on a trip to a Scottish mill and press-ganged a woman on the train home into teaching me to knit. A few months later I was so hooked that I put away my paintbrushes and proceeded to knit myself a career. *Glorious Knitting* was published in 1986.

Needlepoint entered my life in a similarly unexpected way. Lady Harlech, who was working for Vogue magazine at the time, asked me to design a needlepoint cushion

ABOVE TOP Liza and me sitting in front of my still-life that proved an irresistible omen that I was to do a patchwork book. ABOVE Peter Adler's exciting antique quilt inspired my Super Triangles knitted jacket. LEFT Liza took my knitted jacket and translated it into the Super Triangles Quilt (see page 50 for instructions).

cover for her to stitch. I painted a paper-weight on needlepoint canvas, and to show her where various colours would go, I stitched a bit in each section of the design. Before I knew it I had finished the whole cushion cover and went on to try other designs. A few years later I had amassed a body of work that became my second book – *Glorious Needlepoint*.

Patchwork happened to me in an even stranger fashion. When I was promoting my books in America, I was introduced to Liza Prior Lucy who was a representative for Rowan Yarns in the New York City area. She was one of the first enthusiasts to spread the word about my books and designs to her customers. On one of my promotion tours, Liza started telling me how excited she was about her new patchwork, what a great group of people she was meeting who did it, and how amazingly well stocked the quilt fabric shops were all across the States. She urged me to do a book on patchwork. I listened with half an ear, feeling that knitting and needlepoint (and newer fascinations with rag rugs and mosaics) left me little time to explore a new obsession.

One day, to break through my uncooperative state, Liza created patchwork blocks using the colours and shapes of two of my knitting designs. She sent these to me and I was sufficiently interested to ask for more ideas without actually committing myself to any working plan. She set about translating two more of my patterns and mailed them to me. These were even better, and I began to dream of them as larger quilts but was still very preoccupied with so many other irons in the fire.

Then something occurred that was to prove an irresistible sign that this was indeed a path for me to start down. One morning

Liza received a call in her Pennsylvania home from someone who had purchased a large still-life from me in my painting years. She said she was changing her decor and had heard that Liza might be interested in purchasing an early Kaffe Fassett painting. Liza asked what the subject matter was and nearly choked when she was told it was objects on a patchwork quilt! Later that day she was the proud owner of my best painting of that period, the late 70s.

When I visited Liza on my next trip to the States and saw this familiar work, it brought back my intense love for old quilts. Many of my early still-lifes feature patchworks, and one of my most popular knitting designs, the Super Triangles Jacket, was inspired by an old quilt owned by my friend Peter Adler, a tribal art dealer. The fact that this favourite painting of mine should end up with Liza who was so keen to work with me on a patchwork book seemed too strong an omen to ignore.

I knew enough about patchwork by that time to know it was an exacting kind of work that I would find a little tedious to do properly, so was delighted that Liza would be able and willing to sew into finished quilts the fabrics that I would choose and arrange. As our collaboration developed, she began to see the saturation of colour that I was after and was able to fill in gaps that always occur when one collaborates from afar as we were forced to do, with me in London, and Liza in New Hope, Pennsylvania.

At first there were definite wrong choices of fabric that only became clear when I would view the finished piece on a visit to plan further quilts. Several patches would have to be painstakingly removed from dodgey blocks in the quilts. Sometimes Liza

Above The Patchwork Rose needlepoint cushion kit was designed just after my first trip to Guatemala. Facing page My Pink Roman Blocks patchwork (left) inspired me to design the Roman Blocks knitted crew neck (top right) and the Roman Blocks needlepoint cushion (bottom right). (See page 159 for needlepoint kit information.)

would make up blocks and mail them to me to assemble and check on discordant notes. Other times I was able to use tea dye to soften a harsh white ground of a colour that was too light, thus saving the unpicking of a block to remove a contrasting maverick element.

As the book progressed, I felt more and more of an urge to travel to Liza's work-room in the States where her vast collection of fabrics begged to be assembled into kaleidoscopes of colourful patterns. To begin with, we used the floor to assemble patches and studied the arrangements with the aid of a quilter's reducing glass. Then a tiny white board in Liza's sewing room allowed us to view the arranged patches propped up perpendicularly.

As our ideas gathered pace so did my desire to see a whole quilt arranged before it was sewn, in order to eliminate the worst gaffs in design. Liza then devised a much larger board covered with camel-coloured flannel that we could stick the fabric pieces to. This way we could see at a glance the whole ensemble to judge the level of contrast and movement of colour.

As usual with a new medium to explore, patchwork geometry has spilled its inspiration back into my other activities. I have done a whole knitting collection for Rowan Yarn based on patchwork patterns called

California Patches and designed several needlepoints also on the same theme, including the Roman Blocks cushion (above) and the Patchwork Rose cushion (facing page).

I feel this first collection of patchwork is just the beginning of a new adventure. Some of the quilts have come close to my vision, while others would be entirely different if I had time to start over. I look forward to seeing personal interpretations of these basic ideas and know from observation that most quilters will do their own thing with great confidence.

Soft Pastels

Sugared almonds, party dresses, antique paper roses, and old English chintzes flooded my mind with softness as I started the designs for this chapter. Visions of elegant, flowery Japanese teacups and subtle, embroidered silks conjured up the satin touch and froth of flower petals. I wanted to recreate in my pastel patchworks my first impressions of grand old English drawing rooms with threadbare drapes and couch covers in blowzy rose prints. After being brought up with the typical bright, crisp clean-cut American colour schemes, I had quickly warmed to the relaxed, friendly feel of the English country houses. In their spacious rooms, fading shades, frayed edges and occasional stains add a patina that saves pastels from being too cloyingly sweet. The older and softer my pastel patchworks get, the more appealing they should become. They are easy to live with, yet intricate enough to reveal shadowy depths as the years pass by.

FACING PAGE I loved painting this still-life of floral pottery arranged on an old 1930s quilt (top left), which is so like my Frothy Table Cover with cakes and flowery china (top right). A lovely striped dish captures the mood of the Pinafore-print Quilt (bottom left), and Steve Lovi's 1980s photograph of Designers Guild wallpaper sets the pastel mood perfectly (bottom right).

Pastel is for me an extreme. Often when I am putting a pastel colour scheme together, I hear the comment 'Oh, that's too sweet for me', or 'I'm not a flowery sort of person'. I didn't think that I was either until I experienced the Oriental brand of floweriness. Having been shocked and delighted at the sets of cherry blossoms, sweet blue skies and over-rouged cheeks in Japanese and Chinese theatre, I started playing with this heightened frilliness in my own work. Easter with its similar high palette of blues, pinks and pale yellows makes me aware every year of the therapeutic quality of colour.

I remember once visiting a Trinidadian friend in his London flat in the overcast leaden grey of English winter. As I opened his door, the whole room danced with gleeful high colour. Every vase, pot and glass was stuffed with plastic flowers of brilliant yellows, lavenders and pinks. After recovering from the shock of plastic flowers (a definite no-no during my Californian upbringing), I shared his glee and the sunny effect he was creating in a cold, northern clime.

So often the kitsch, vulgar seaside aspect of cheap design inspires me – budgerigars, working-class funerals, end-of-pier candy shops, market stalls selling little girl's party dresses, and flowery cups and saucers in old lady bric-a-brac shops. I once saw a tea shop in the West of Ireland where every cake plate and cup and saucer had a flowery pattern, but none matched. I smiled happily all the way home at the childish delight and confidence of those table settings.

The quilting shops are making this world of piecing fabric a very rewarding experience indeed. Just walking through the shops with rows of variations on colour and pattern is enough to make the dullest type start to fizzle with ideas. When I was shopping

ABOVE The Pinafore-print Diamonds Quilt in an elegant old-world English bedroom that has a leafy theme. LEFT The instructions for this Pinafore-print Diamonds patchwork are on page 76.

for the Pinafore-print Diamonds patchwork (above and left), I was exploding with excitement as I laid one flower print on another, knowing that these pastel prints were going to slot into each other like facets of a diamond. The three attendants in Washington DC's G-Street fabric store got the buzz and shared my enthusiasm. The bolts of soft lavender and blue flower prints together on the counter looked for all the world like a stack of old-fashioned ladies'

ABOVE The Pale Floating Blocks Tablecloth in a little gem of a garden house at the American Museum in Bath. RIGHT The Pastel 2-by-2 Quilt. PAGES 18 AND 19 (left to right) The Pastel, Leafy and Tawny versions of the Rosy Quilt.

aprons – hence the name. I also call this design 'Little old Ladies Shelling Peas' because of my vivid childhood memories of merry ladies in flower-dappled aprons sitting shelling peas on the back porches. The finished quilt has the mood of a flowery tiled wall in a Persian bath house.

Pale Floating Blocks (above) is inspired by Steve Lovi's wallpaper boxes on page 12. When I began work on this patchwork, I was just back from Finland where people often decorate in shades of cream, pale grey and white to maximize light on long winter evenings. The idea of Scandinavian off-white and pale blueness flooded my mind, and I could just see the washed white room

the design could go into. The secret to the success of this patchwork was to keep the fabrics faded and pale enough. Several medium colours were eliminated from the first attempt at the design because they were too dark and appeared to poke a hole in the delicate balance. The overall surface should look as if it is being seen through an off-white veil (see page 95 for instructions).

The Pastel 2-by-2 Quilt (right) is the patchwork design that has come the closest to matching my original vision. The warm beige base makes such a soft ground on which to float the medium-toned colours. It was interesting to see how the structure of the chequerboard blocks got totally lost when sewn together (see page 132 for instructions). The lack of any real contrast makes for defused pastelness; light and dark strips of diamonds appear then disperse.

The harmony of the dusty colours in the Pastel 2-by-2 comes close to that of the historic quilts in museums. Because of the subtlety of the quilt's tones it very difficult to capture in a photograph the impact the design has in real life. I finally draped it on my marbleized chest of drawers and the colours radiated quietly.

Once I had agreed to work on this book, Pastel Rosy (see page 18) was the first patchwork I designed from scratch. In my mind was a faded old linen quilt of rose prints I had seen in Wales in the 70s. I picked a series of large-scale floral prints and an equal amount of small-scale close-toned prints. One of these was a deep ochre, which added a lively note and more contrast to the overall dustiness of the palette.

I then went on to create two more totally different moods with the same patchwork layout of squares and checkerboards (see page 68 for Rosy Quilt instructions).

Little Bricks Baby Quilt

Fortunately, many of the elegant, old classic shirt stripings have been revived in present-day fabric collections, making it is possible to create today a mellow statement like the Little Bricks Baby Quilt.

The layout of this patchwork is based on African strip-weaving in which narrow strips of fabric are woven and then sewn together end-to-end and side-by-side to form large pieces of fabric. Many of the most popular of these narrow African strips are stripes of all descriptions. This simple patchwork structure of rectangles, or 'bricks', is an easy one to play with.

You know that different stripes piled together create an exciting effect when you spot a pile of shirtings on bolts in a shop or market. I have really lit up in the past when I have spotted striped mattresses piled on trucks in outdoor markets in Guatemala and India. They use wonderful bold stripes in the same chalky colours seen on canvas deck chairs (see page 12).

The Navy Bricks Quilt is a darker version of the same patchwork layout (see photograph on page 93).

Size of quilt

The finished Little Bricks Baby Quilt measures 34in x 46in (87cm x 115cm). The Navy Bricks version measures 86in x 90in (210cm x 225cm). *Note that the metric sizes will not exactly match the imperial sizes and that the tying or quilting will slightly reduce the final measurements.*

LEFT There is a delicious play of stripes on the Little Bricks Quilt on the bed and the Pale Floating Blocks hanging on the wall. The Handkerchief-patch Curtain is made of flea-market handkerchiefs.

Little Bricks colour recipe

This scheme is reminiscent of the old faded colours of men's shirting and handkerchiefs. The patch fabrics are narrow woven stripes. The rectangular patches with lengthways stripes are a variety of fabrics (and a few plaids) in blue and ecru and in blue on grey (fabric A). The rectangular patches with widthways stripes are fabrics mostly in ochres, dusty pinks, rusts and sages (fabric B). The border fabric is a simple floral print of rust on ecru.

Alternate colour recipe

Navy Bricks (page 93): The patch fabrics are a mixture of printed and woven stripes. The rectangular patches with lengthways stripes are a few different fabrics in dark blue and ecru (fabric A). The patches with widthways stripes are a variety of fabrics mostly in blues, lavenders, golds, olives, and reds from maroons to pinks (fabric B).

The border fabric is one of the rust fabrics with turquoise and green stripes. SPECIAL NOTE Where the directions for the Navy Bricks version differ from those of the Little Bricks version, they are given in square brackets.

Materials

44–45in (112cm) wide 100% cotton fabrics:
• *Fabric A:* ¼yd (25cm) [1½yd (1.4m)] each of at least 8[3] different striped fabrics
• *Fabric B:* ¼yd (25cm) [¾yd (70cm)] or more each of at least 8[5] different striped fabrics
• *Border fabric:* ½yd (45cm) [1½yd (1.4m)]

ASSEMBLY FOR LITTLE BRICKS BABY QUILT

Key

patch with
lengthways stripes
in fabric A

patch with
widthways stripes
in fabric B

O = Tie here

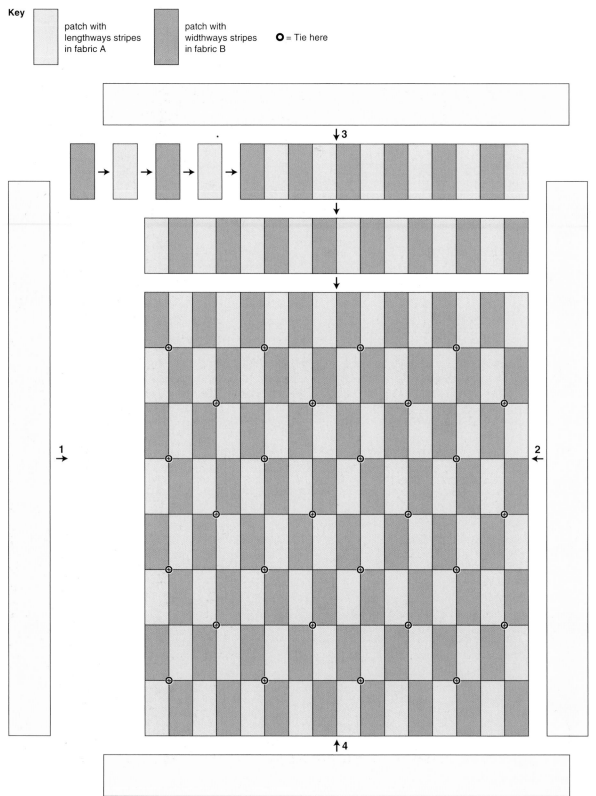

- *Backing fabric:* $1\frac{1}{2}$ yd (1.4m) [$5\frac{1}{2}$ yd (5m)]
- *Outer-binding fabric:* $\frac{1}{2}$ yd (45cm) [$\frac{3}{4}$ yd (70cm)] of a blue-and-ecru stripe

Plus the following materials:

- Wool or polyester batting [cotton batting], at least 3in (7.5cm) larger all

ABOVE Use this Little Bricks colour scheme or the Navy version on page 93.

around than the finished pieced quilt top
• One ball of ecru wool yarn for tying the layers together [orange cotton quilting thread for the widthways striped patches and navy cotton quilting thread for the lengthways striped patches]

ASSEMBLY FOR NAVY BRICKS QUILT

Key
 patch with lengthways stripes in fabric A   patch with widthways stripes in fabric B

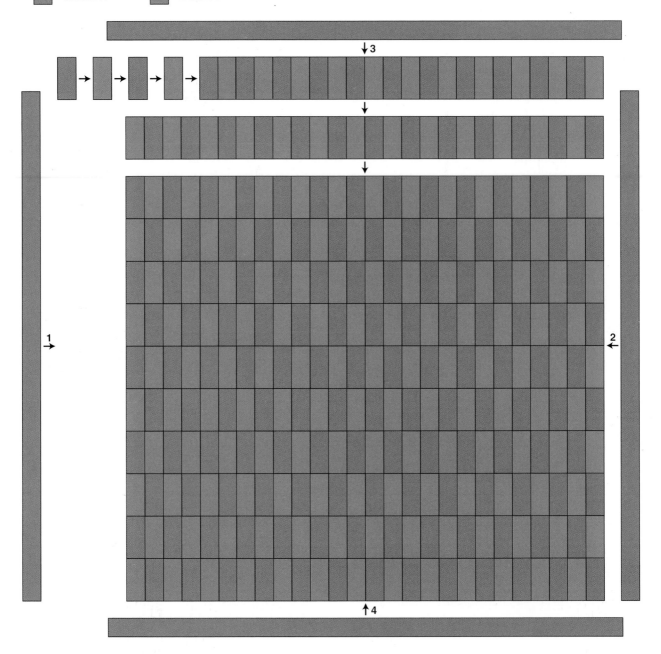

Patch shapes

The centre of each of the Bricks quilts is made from rectangular patches that are all the same size. The finished rectangular patch for the Little Bricks version measures 1¾in x 4in (4.5cm x 10cm) [the finished rectangular patch for the Navy Bricks measures 3in x 7in (7.5cm x 17.5cm)].

Cutting

Fabric A: cut 80 rectangles 2¼in x 4½in (6cm x 11.5cm) [cut 156 rectangles 3½in x 7½in (9cm x 19cm)] so that the stripes run down the length of the patch.

Fabric B: cut 80 rectangles 2¼in x 4½in (6cm x 11.5cm) [cut 156 rectangles 3½in x 7½in (9cm x 19cm)] so that the stripes run across the width of the patch.

Border strips: cut 2 strips $3^{1}/_{2}$ in x $40^{1}/_{2}$ in (9cm x 101.5cm) [$3^{1}/_{2}$ in x $84^{1}/_{2}$ in (9cm x 211.5cm), piecing if necessary] for the side borders, and 2 strips $3^{1}/_{2}$ in x $34^{1}/_{2}$ in (9cm x 88.5cm) [$3^{1}/_{2}$ in x $84^{1}/_{2}$ in (9cm x 211.5cm), piecing if necessary] for the top and bottom borders.

SPECIAL NOTE The cutting sizes include the seam allowance.

Assembling the patches

Following the diagram on page 22 for the Little Bricks [on page 24 for the Navy Bricks], arrange the rectangles in 10 [12] separate rows of 16 [26] patches, alternating the lengthways and widthways stripes.

When assembling the quilt, use a $^{1}/_{4}$ in (7.5mm) seam allowance throughout. Join the patches together in rows, sewing together along the long sides. Then join the rows together.

Making the border

Following the diagram, join on the two side borders first, then join on the bottom and top borders.

Finishing the quilt

Press the assembled quilt top before beginning the tying or quilting.

For the Little Bricks version, layer the quilt top, batting and backing (see page

QUILTING

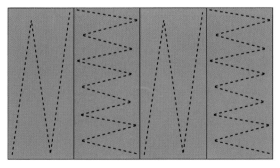

ABOVE Liza made up this quizzical little teddy bear from the striped offcuts of the Pale Floating Blocks Tablecloth (see page 16).

147). Then using a 10in (25cm) length of yarn, tie through the layers at the spots indicated on the chart. Trim the ends of the yarn to a suitable length (see page 148 for instructions on how to tie quilts).

For the Navy Bricks version, layer the quilt top, batting and backing, and baste together (see page 147). As indicated on the quilting diagram (left), quilt each lengthways-striped patch with a lengthways zigzag line using navy quilting thread, and each widthways-striped patch with a widthways zigzag line using orange thread.

For both versions, trim the quilt edge. Then cut the binding strips on the bias from the striped binding fabric and attach (see page 148).

Herringbone Baby Quilt

Taking the leftover diamonds from the Pinafore-print Diamonds Quilt (see pages 14 and 15), I devised the Herringbone Baby Quilt with its very three-dimensional pattern. The light-dark in-and-out illusion is created by taking the right side of the bright pastel fabrics as the dark side of the herringbone pattern and flipping them to the wrong side to create the pale side. This technique reminded me of a trip to Hawaii when the fashion in Hawaiian shirts was to use the wrong side of the fabric for a soft faded look.

The Herringbone Baby Quilt was shot in a friend's rustic garden house with her sensational collection of granny-square blankets and her stencilled patchwork floor. Doesn't all that geometry work a treat together?

Although the quilt was designed in a small size, you could easily enlarge it by adding more double rows of diamonds widthways and more zigzag rows lengthways (see the diagram for the quilt assembly on page 28).

Size of quilt

The finished patchwork quilt measures $49\frac{1}{2}$in x 59in (126cm x 150cm). *Note that the quilting will slightly reduce the final measurements.*

Colour recipe

The diamond-template fabrics are small- and medium-scale floral prints with flowers, mostly in pinks and mauves on backgrounds in sweet blues, lavenders and aquas. The right side of these fabrics is used for the brighter tones and the wrong side for the muted tones.

The borders are prints with small- and medium-scale pink flowers on a variety of medium-blue backgrounds.

Materials

44–45in (112cm) wide 100% cotton fabrics:
• *Diamond-template fabrics:* $\frac{3}{4}$yd (70cm) or more each of 10 different small- and medium-scale floral prints in the colours outlined in the *Colour Recipe*
• *Border fabric:* scrap strips of at least three different small- and medium-scale floral prints with pink flowers on medium-blue backgrounds
• *Backing fabric:* 3yd (2.8m)
• *Outer-binding fabric:* $\frac{1}{2}$yd (45cm) of a small-scale floral print with blue flowers on a pink background
Plus the following materials:
• Cotton batting, at least 3in (7.5cm) larger all around than the finished pieced quilt top
• Light blue cotton quilting thread

Patch Shapes

The centre of the quilt is made from four patch shapes – a whole diamond (template A), a half diamond (template C), a quarter diamond (template D) and a reverse quarter diamond (D reverse).

The actual-size templates are given on page 150.

The four borders are made from $2\frac{1}{2}$in (6.5cm) wide strips of random lengths.

LEFT The Herringbone Baby Quilt in an enchanted rustic garden house with its stencilled floor and a glorious collection of granny blankets.

QUILT ASSEMBLY

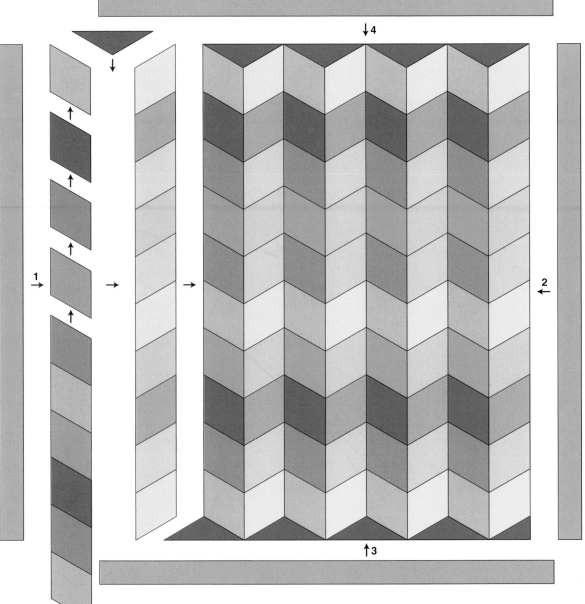

Cutting

Template A: cut 10 whole diamonds from 10 different fabrics (a total of 100 diamonds), plus a few extra random prints for the 'mistake' patches.

Template C: cut 8 half diamonds from the mostly blue fabrics.

Template D and D reverse: cut one quarter diamond and one reverse quarter diamond from the blue fabrics as for C patches.

Border strips: cut random lengths of $2^{1}/_{2}$ in (6.5cm) wide strips from a few of the blue fabrics as described in the *Colour Recipe* on page 27 for a total of at least $6^{1}/_{4}$ yd (5.7m) in length.

TEMPLATES

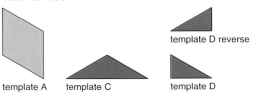

template A   template C   template D reverse   template D

ABOVE The right side and the wrong side of the fabrics alternate to create the three-dimensional look in the Herringbone Baby Quilt.

SPECIAL NOTE If you are marking seam lines on your patches, remember that for five patches out of the 10 template-A patches from each fabric set, the wrong side of the fabric becomes the 'right side'. (See pages for detailed information on using templates and on marking and cutting template patches.)

Arranging the diamonds

Following the diagram on the opposite page, take 10 diamonds cut from the same fabric and arrange them in a horizontal row, with the first diamond on the left-hand side of the row right side up, the second wrong side up, and so on so that the right-side-up and wrong-side-up patches alternate.

Arrange 10 more horizontal rows in the same way, occasionally replacing a diamond with a 'mistake' diamond of the same intensity but of a different fabric print.

Assembling the diamonds

When assembling the quilt, use the seam allowance marked on the templates throughout. Following the diagram, join the diamonds together in 10 vertical rows, then join the rows together.

Using a set-in seam technique, sew the half diamonds across the top and bottom of the quilt with the right side of the fabric on the right side of the quilt. Then sew the two quarter diamonds to the two lower corners of the quilt.

Making the border

Join together end-to-end the $2\frac{1}{2}$ in (6.5cm) wide border strips. Then cut from the joined strips, two side border pieces measuring $54\frac{1}{2}$ in (138.5cm) long and a top and bottom piece each measuring $49\frac{1}{2}$ in (126cm) long.

Join on the two side borders first, then join on the bottom and top borders.

Finishing the quilt

Press the assembled quilt top. Layer the top, batting and backing, and baste together (see page 147). Then quilt with outline quilting by stitching $\frac{1}{4}$ in (6mm) from each patch seam line as shown below.

Trim the quilt edge and attach the outer binding (see page 148).

QUILTING

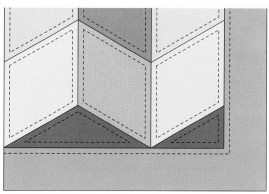

Frothy Table Cover

The Frothy Table Cover is what the pastel chapter is all about for me – lashings of overblown and delicate flowers and glowing fruits against luminous blues and peach tones. This patchwork creates an instant party mood and cries out for pretty floral china and decorated cakes. It would be a wonderful finishing touch for a room decked in rosy wallpaper and frilly curtains.

The angles created by the bluish patches in the overall pattern remind me of old hat boxes and Easter decorations. Liza aptly calls this concoction 'Garden Party in a Blender'.

For a recent exhibition in Japan, I plastered the walls with dozens of Sandersons' most rosy wallpapers and collaged them together in a giant checkerboard. The effect made an energetic texture to show my work against. It also made me see that a very rich, deeper version of these pastel flowers could be created by going to the other extreme and having some rose fabrics with black, maroon and deep cobalt grounds.

Size of table cover

The finished patchwork top measures 88in x 88in (224cm x 224cm). *Note that the metric size will not exactly match the imperial size and that the quilting will slightly reduce the final measurements.*

Colour recipe

The fabrics used are large-scale floral prints at least half of which should be voluptuous roses if possible. There are two colour groups: fabric A is basically cool florals on grey-blue, sky blue, aqua, periwinkle and soft green grounds, and fabric B is predominantly warm pink florals on pale peach, cream and café-au-lait grounds.

The border fabric for this design (fabric C) has bold periwinkle-blue, rose-pink, sage and yellow stripes.

Materials

44–45in (112cm) wide 100% cotton fabrics:
- *Fabric A:* $\frac{1}{4}$ yd (25cm) or more each of at least 13 different blue and green floral prints
- *Fabric B:* $\frac{1}{4}$ yd (25cm) or more each of at least 13 different pink floral prints
- *Fabric C (border):* $1\frac{1}{4}$ yd (1.2m) of a bold striped fabric, with stripes running parallel to selvedge

Plus the following materials:
- *Backing fabric:* piece of cotton flannel at least 90in (230cm) square
- Cotton quilting thread

Patch shapes

The centre of the patchwork table cover is made from right-angled triangles. Because the triangular patches are cut from squares, no template is necessary.

Cutting

Fabric A: cut 50 squares $8\frac{7}{8}$ in x $8\frac{7}{8}$ in (22.5cm x 22.5cm), then cut each square in half diagonally to form 100 right-angled triangles.

Fabric B: cut 50 squares $8\frac{7}{8}$ in x $8\frac{7}{8}$ in (22.5cm x 22.5cm), then cut each square in half diagonally to form 100 right-angled triangles.

Fabric C: cut 8 strips $4\frac{1}{2}$ in (11.5cm) wide by the length of the fabric, so the stripes run lengthways on the strips.

RIGHT Tea is served! The Frothy Table Cover dancing with pastel cakes, flowers and porcelain.

BLOCK ASSEMBLY

TABLE COVER ASSEMBLY

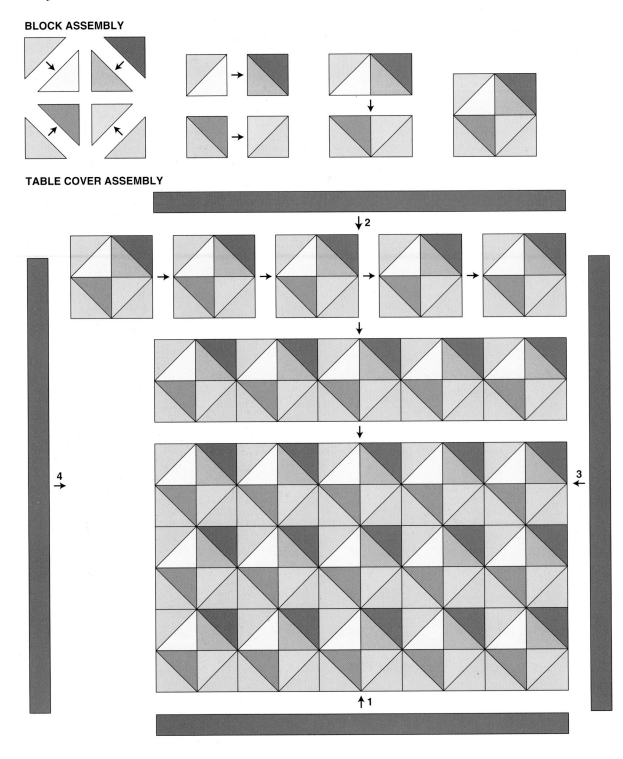

SPECIAL NOTE The cutting sizes include the seam allowance.

Making the blocks

Select four different fabric-A triangles and four different fabric-B triangles for each block. Using a $^1/_4$ in (7mm) seam allowance throughout, make four squares, each with one fabric-A triangle and one fabric-B triangle. Join two squares together, then the remaining two squares together. To complete the block, join the two rows together with the fabric-B triangles at the centre. Make a total of 25 blocks in the same way.

ABOVE The Frothy colour scheme is made up of a warm group of voluptuous pink florals and a cool group of blue and green florals (see Colour Recipe on page 31).

Assembling the blocks

Arrange the 25 blocks into five rows of five blocks. Join the patches together in rows, then join the rows together.

Making the border

Sew two fabric-C strips together for each side of the quilt. Trim two of the joined strips to $80^{1}/_{2}$ in (204cm) long and the remaining two to $88^{1}/_{2}$ in (225cm). Join the two shorter strips to the top and bottom of the centre panel. Then join the longer strips to the sides.

Finishing the table cover

Press the assembled patchwork. Layer the patchwork top and the flannel backing and baste together (see page 147). Quilt with stitch-in-the-ditch quilting. Fold the seam allowances along the outside edge to the inside and top stitch close to the edge. Top stitch again $^{1}/_{4}$ in (7mm) from the edge.

Circus

The excitement of dancing jugglers, refracting colour, music, and barkers – this chapter spells party time! The circus with its undulating, decorated carousel horses and agile, loudly dressed clowns is a world of contrasts, bright optimistic colour and carnival gaiety. When I think of circuses, I conjure up a world of Victorian poster art and, even further back to commedia dell'arte, costumes of deep rose pink and apple-green stripes, Pierrot figures in diamonds of yellow, red and turquoise, crazy-patch jackets and waistcoats. Predominant in my vision are great tents of bold contrasting stripes and strong patterns, such as fan shapes, polka dots and flags – all made to reach out and captivate an excited audience. Patchwork using these bright contrasting tones is in its element. It is the perfect medium for boldly striped curtains, tented ceilings, banners to announce a party or exhibition, and dynamic draped tablecloths for an instant party mood.

FACING PAGE Here are stripes in many guises to introduce the Circus mood – English deck chairs photographed by Steve Lovi (top left), the striped boldness of the carousel roof in the early twentieth-century painting *All the Fun of the Fair* by Ernest Proctor (top right), a detail of my Circus Tents Wall Hanging (bottom left) and striped fabrics in the Super Triangles Baby Quilt (bottom right).

ABOVE The brilliant tones of the Zinnia 2-by-2 are set off by the bright china and flowers. FACING PAGE The Citrus and Delft 2-by-2 Quilt (top) and Blue Roman Blocks Quilt (bottom) hanging on the porch of a rustic cottage (see pages 132 and 99 for instructions).

The Zinnia 2-by-2 Quilt (above) perfectly embodies the exotic atmosphere and optimistic colours of the Circus mood that I was trying to create in the patchwork collection for this chapter. Both the quilt's name and its reds and oranges were inspired by a bouquet of zinnias I bought at a farm produce shop in Pennsylvania. I mentioned to Liza that the dusty pinks, intense scarlets and oranges of the zinnias with their fresh green leaves would make a knockout patchwork colour scheme. You pull the fabrics and I'll get sewing right away, she challenged, even though we had decided we had more than enough projects on the go for this book.

The Zinnia design fell together with great ease and enjoyment thanks to Liza's vast collection of fabrics. We added the bow-tie shapes to the basic 2-by-2 layout because so many of the bold bright patterns I was picking made me think of clowns' bow ties!

Wanting to make a blue-and-white version of the 2-by-2 quilt, I visited a friend in the south of England to see how she had dealt with the blue-and-white theme in her imaginative interiors. She decorates the way I dream — a very rare lavish eye she possesses, taking each theme in her house to delicious extremes. She didn't let me down! I found walls of intense lemon yellow and everywhere strong deep cobalt blue and white — mosaics around the fireplace, a great variety of blue-and-white fabrics on couches, cushions and rugs, and most delightful of all, a profusion of plates up the chimney and around the room creating an amazingly original three-dimensional border.

With these visions fresh in my mind, I rushed to America to have Liza create the Citrus and Delft 2-by-2 Table Cover (right and page 2). Luckily, I was able to find a dark cobalt blue and white paisley-like fabric that figures as a constant throughout the patchwork. I thought I might have gone too contrasty in my colours until I took the finished piece to my English friend's room where it settled in quite comfortably.

A more geometric version of tumbling blocks, Roman Blocks (below) is a dream layout to play with. The structure is from a Roman mosaic in very close tones of neutral beiges. I was aiming at a dusty blueness with accents of plum and turquoise. The dark border and taupe background give this quilt a quiet elegance that makes it the calmest piece in this jazzy chapter.

Pink and Blue Pennants

Flags fluttering in many colours – what could be jollier? Seeing flags on boats, around party marquees or at funfairs always gives me a boost. I hope this dance of pointed shapes does the same for you.

My first version of the Pennants pattern was the Yellow Pennants, drenched with sun and dancing with lively colour. Knowing that some might not share my passion for yellows, I dreamed up the slightly cooler Pink and Blue version. All the colours in it are slightly dusty so that they harmonize well together, but have just enough light-dark contrast to show off the jaunty points.

The Pennants Quilt formula is a good one to try for any colour scheme. Shades of soft greys could be used in place of yellows for instance, or warm terracotta browns with the same group of bright shades as the Yellow Pennants; the effect would be very Santa Fé desert bright.

Size of quilt

The finished Pink and Blue Pennants Quilt measures $66\frac{1}{2}$ in x $78\frac{1}{2}$ in (169cm x 200cm). The Yellow Pennants version is the same size. *Note that the quilting will slightly reduce the final measurements.*

Pink and Blue Pennants colour recipe

The fabrics used are small-scale multi-coloured and monochromatic prints, mini-plaids and stripes. The colour in the blocks in the quilt centre are divided into two tone groups – deep tones and medium tones. The deep tones are mostly browny ochres, oranges, plums, teal and kingfisher blues, with a smattering of rusts, reds and purples; and the medium tones are oranges, pinks, butterscotch, lime, aquas and blues.

The colours for the inner border are deep browny ochres and burgundies; for the outer border, pinks, blues and oranges.

Alternative colour recipe

Yellow Pennants (page 39): The fabrics used are small-scale multi-coloured and monochromatic prints, French country prints, polka dots, mini-plaids and stripes.

The colours used for the blocks in the quilt centre are divided into two groups. One group includes yellows (from high yellow to mellow ochre); and the other group includes high pastels and brilliant jewel tones – magenta, bright pinks, salmon, brilliant orange, lime, apple greens, baby blues and turquoise.

The colours for the inner border are half creams (off-whites to pale yellows) and half deep yellows. The colours for the outer border are divided into three colour groups – yellows, greens and blues, and pinks and oranges. The colours for the prairie-points edging are the same three colour groups as those for the outer border. SPECIAL NOTE Where the directions for the Yellow Pennants version differ from those of the Pink and Blue Pennants version, they are given in square brackets.

Materials

44–45in (112cm) wide 100% cotton fabrics:
• *Patch fabrics:* scraps of an assortment of fabrics, with at least half of the scraps in

PAGES 38 AND 39 The Yellow Pennants Quilt.
RIGHT The Pink and Blue Pennants Quilt, with the Super Triangles Quilt hanging in the corner.

pinks and browny ochres [yellows]
• *Backing fabric:* 4yd (3.7m)
• *Outer-binding fabric:* ¾yd (70cm) of a burgundy and rust stripe [a yellow small-scale print]
Plus the following materials:
• Lightweight cotton batting, at least 3in (7.5cm) larger all around than pieced quilt
• Cotton quilting thread

Patch shapes

The quilt centre is made from four blocks that are all the same size. The blocks are made up of triangles that are sewn together using the paper foundation-piecing method. The finished blocks (S, T, S-reverse and T-reverse) measure 6in x 6in (15cm x 15cm).

FOUNDATION-PIECED BLOCKS

block S   block T

block S reverse   block T reverse

FOUNDATION-PIECED INNER-BORDER STRIPS

strip U   strip V

OUTER-BORDER BLOCK ASSEMBLY

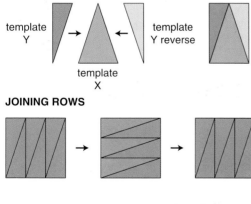

template Y   →   ←   template Y reverse

template X

JOINING ROWS

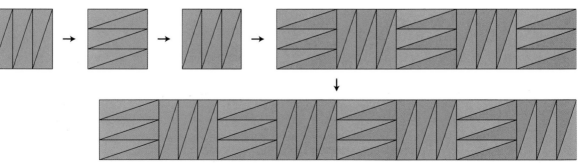

The inner border is made from two different strips that are the same size. The strips are formed from triangles that are sewn together using the foundation-piecing method. The finished strips (U and V) measure 3in x 6in (7.5cm x 15cm).

The outer border is made from three templates – two small triangles (templates Y and Y reverse) and a large triangle (template X). See page 152 for templates.

The prairie-points edging on the Yellow Pennants version is optional and is made from rectanglar and square patches without the use of templates.

Foundation papers

The foundation-papers used for this quilt are given on pages 152 and 153. See pages 146 and 147 for the instructions for foundation piecing. Make the required number of copies of each foundation piece.
Block-S and block-T foundation papers: a total of 40 copies.
Block-S-reverse and block-T-reverse foundation papers: a total of 40 copies.
Strip-U and strip-V foundation papers: a total of 36 copies.
SPECIAL NOTE The 'reverse' blocks are used for the 'horizontal' squares in the quilt centre. To make block-S-reverse and block-T-reverse papers, trace blocks S and T on tracing paper, turn the tracing over and redraw the lines on the wrong side of the

JOINING BORDERS

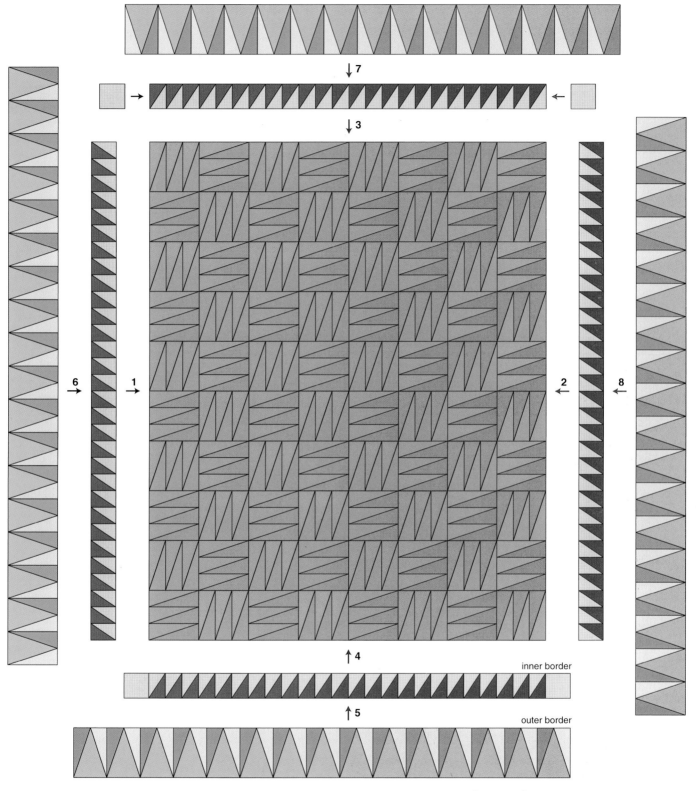

inner border

outer border

paper. Then renumber the triangles from right to left. For the reverse foundation blocks, copy the reversed image that is on the wrong side of the tracing paper.

Cutting pieces for quilt centre

For one colour group, select fabric scraps in the deep tones [in a range of yellows]. For the other colour group, select fabric

ABOVE The Pink and Blue Pennants. See page 39 for the Yellow Pennants version.

scraps in the medium tones [in the high pastels and brilliant jewel tones]. Cut these scraps into 3in–4in (7.5cm–10cm) wide strips of any length. Cut more strips as the foundation blocks are pieced.

Cutting pieces for inner border

Select fabric scraps in deep browny ochres and burgundies [in creams and deep yellows]. Cut these scraps into 3in–4in (7.5cm–10cm) wide strips of any length. Cut more strips as the foundation strips are pieced.

Cut four corner squares measuring $3^{1}/_{2}$ in x $3^{1}/_{2}$ in (9cm x 9cm) from ochre-coloured [cream-coloured] scraps.

Cutting pieces for outer border

Template X: cut 66 triangles from a range of pinks [yellows].

Template Y: cut 66 triangles from a range oranges [pinks and oranges].
Template Y reverse: cut 66 triangles from a range of blues [greens and blues].

Cutting pieces for prairie points

The prairie-points edging is an optional edging for the Yellow Pennants version (see page 39). For the prairie-points, cut 24 squares measuring $6^{1}/_{2}$ in x $6^{1}/_{2}$ in (16.5cm x 16.5cm) from a range of yellows. Then cut 24 rectangles measuring $3^{1}/_{2}$ in x $6^{1}/_{2}$ in (9cm x 16.5cm) from a range of pinks and oranges and 24 rectangles the same size from a range of greens and blues.

Making blocks for the quilt centre

Make the blocks using the foundation papers and following the instructions for foundation piecing on pages 146 and 147. Using two colours for each block (but more than one fabric of each of the two colours), use the deep tones [yellows] for the even-numbered areas and the medium tones [the high pastels and brilliant jewel tones] for the odd-numbered areas. Occasionally, make 'mistakes' and choose an unexpected colour in a block.

Make a total of 40 S- and T-blocks for the 'vertical' blocks, and a total of 40 S-reverse and T-reverse blocks for the 'horizontal' blocks.

Making the inner-border strips

Make the strips using the foundation papers and following the instructions for foundation piecing on pages 146 and 147. Using two colours for each strip, use deep browny ochres [deep yellows] for the even-numbered areas and burgundies [creams] for the odd-numbered areas. Make a total of 36 U- and V-strips.

Making the outer-border blocks

Select a pink [yellow] X-template triangle, an orange [pink or orange] Y-template triangle and a blue [green or blue] Y-reverse template triangle. Join the patches following the outer-border block assembly diagram. Make a total of 66 outer-border blocks in the same way.

Assembling the quilt centre

When assembling the quilt, use the seam allowance marked on the foundation pieces throughout. Following the diagram shown on page 42, arrange the blocks in 10 rows of 8 blocks, alternating 'horizontal' blocks (S and T) with 'vertical' blocks (S-reverse and T-reverse) and placing S and T blocks and S-reverse and T-reverse randomly. Join the blocks together in rows, then join the rows together.

Making the inner border

To make each of the two side borders, join together end-to-end a total of 10 U-strips and V-strips, with all of the ochre [yellow] triangles pointing in the same direction and trying to match similar fabrics next to each other so that it is difficult to see where one strip ends and the next starts. For the top and bottom borders, join together a total of 8 U-strips and V-strips.

Sew the border corners to the ends of the top and bottom borders. With the ochre [yellow] triangles pointing outwards, join the two side borders to the quilt centre, then sew on the top and bottom borders.

Making the outer border

To make each of the two side borders, join together end-to-end 18 outer-border blocks, with all of the pink [yellow] triangles pointing in the same direction. For

PRAIRIE-POINTS EDGING ASSEMBLY

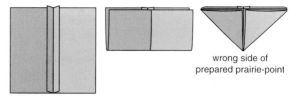

wrong side of prepared prairie-point

PRAIRIE-POINTS EDGING ON YELLOW PENNANTS

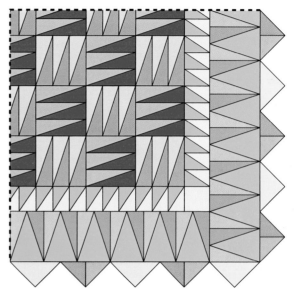

the top and bottom borders, join together 15 outer-border blocks in the same way.

With the pink [yellow] triangles pointing outwards, join the bottom border to the quilt first, lining up the right-hand edge of the outer border with the lower right-hand edge of the corner of the quilt. Next join the left-hand side border strip to the quilt, abutting the bottom edge to the bottom border; then join the seam between the two outer-border pieces. Sew on the top outer border, then the right-hand border in the same way.

Finishing the quilt

Remove the foundation papers and press the quilt top. Layer the quilt top, batting and backing, and baste (see page 147). Quilt in-the-ditch around the points (but not between the blocks) on the quilt centre, along both sides of the inner border and around the points on the outer border. If there is a prairie-points edging, skip to the instructions that follow; if not, attach the binding (see page 148).

Making the prairie-points edging

When making the prairie points, use a $\frac{1}{4}$ in (7.5mm) seam allowance throughout. With wrong sides facing, join a pink or orange rectangle to a green or blue rectangle along the long edges to form a square (see page 45). Press the seam open. With the wrong side facing upwards and the pink (orange) fabric on the left, fold the square in half widthways. Press the fold. Then fold each of the lower corners up to meet at the centre top with the raw edges aligned. Press both folds. Make 24 two-tone points in the same way.

Then make 24 yellow prairie points in the same way as the two-tone points.

Lay the quilt right side up. With the right sides facing and the raw edges aligned, pin 6 yellow and 7 two-toned prairie points to each side edge of the quilt, and 6 yellow and 5 two-toned points to the top and bottom edges, alternating the two-toned and yellow points.

Cut the 2in (5cm) wide strips for the binding and join them together end-to-end to make a continuous strip at least $8\frac{1}{4}$ yd (7.5m) long. Fold the strip in half lengthways with the wrong sides together and press. Pin the doubled binding on top of the prairie points aligning the raw edges, and baste through all the layers. Machine stitch. Remove the basting.

Turn the points to the outside and fold the binding over the raw edge. Mitring the binding at the corners, sew the folded edge of the binding to the wrong side of the quilt and press.

ABOVE The Yellow Stripes Cushion against a wardrobe I painted for the Kaffe Fassett Designs shop in Bath, England. On the floor, my hooked rag rug of diamonds and the Venetian Tile Cushion (see page 110 for the Venetian Tile patchwork).

Yellow Stripes Cushion

The stripes on this cushion create a weave effect. Although we have used yellow and peachy tones, you could use any other colours of stripes for a similar effect. It would be most striking in sharp contrasting colours, even black and white. The darkest tones in the Yellow Stripes Cushion are striped fabrics that I designed for Oxfam to be produced in India (see page 92).

I once designed a random stripe fabric and had it sewn together in blocks of four squares cut with the stripes on the diagonal.

CUSHION COVER ASSEMBLY

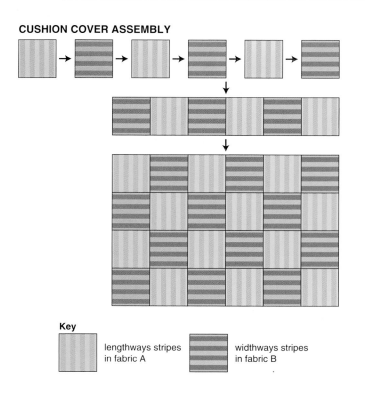

Key

lengthways stripes
in fabric A

widthways stripes
in fabric B

The effect created was a bit like the Mexican god's eyes – concentric diamonds radiating out from the centre. I then made an exciting checkerboard design by sewing the blocks together with solid-coloured squares to isolate each of the diamonds. You could use this as an alternative idea for your cushion cover and make it in the same colours as the Yellow Stripes (see _Colour Recipe_ below).

Size of cushion

The finished patchwork cushion cover measures 18in x 18in (45cm x 45cm). _Note that the metric size will not exactly match the imperial size._

Colour recipe

The patches with lengthways stripes are cut from two-colour striped fabrics with yellow-gold grounds (fabric A). The patches with widthways stripes are cut from a variety of stripe patterns in dusty medium tones (fabric B).

Materials

44–45in (112cm) wide 100% cotton fabric:
• _Fabric A:_ scraps of at least two different woven stripes in the colours outlined in the _Colour Recipe_
• _Fabric B:_ scraps of at least four different woven stripes in the colours outlined in the _Colour Recipe_
• _Backing fabric:_ ³⁄4 yd (70cm)
Plus the following materials:
• 18in (45cm) square cushion (pillow form)
• Matching sewing thread
• 16in (40cm) zipper (optional)

Patch shape

The cushion cover is made from a single size of square patch. The finished patch measures 3in (7.5cm) square.

Cutting

Cut 36 squares measuring 3¹⁄2 in x 3¹⁄2 in (9cm x 9cm).
SPECIAL NOTE The cutting size includes the seam allowance.

Assembling the patches

When assembling the patchwork cover, use a ¹⁄4 in (7.5mm) seam allowance through-out. Arrange the patches in 6 rows of 6 squares, positioning them so that the lengthways and widthways stripes alternate. Join the patches together in rows, then join the rows together.

Finishing the cushion cover

Press the patchwork. Cut a backing to the same size. With the right sides facing, stitch the backing to the patchwork, leaving an opening or inserting a zipper in one seam, as desired. Turn right side out and insert the cushion. Stitch the opening closed or simply close the zipper.

Crazy Squares Cushion and Table Runner

Liza spotted a pattern detail in one of my paintings and tried it as a patchwork with great results – the Crazy Squares Cushion and Table Runner. The textile that I had painted was a roughly knitted scarf picked up in the flea market for a couple of dollars. Its bright contrasting colours have featured in several of my paintings. This one was a sketch for a large woven tapestry by the Edinburgh Tapestry Weavers.

Size of table runner and cushion

The finished patchwork table runner measures $16^1/_2$ in x $80^1/_2$ in (42cm x 204.5cm) and the finished patchwork cushion cover measures 16in x 16in (41cm x 41cm). *Note that the quilting will slightly reduce the final measurements of the table runner.*

Colour recipe

The fabrics used for both the table runner and the cushion cover are mostly small-scale monochromatic prints with a few mini-checks and a few two- or three-colour small-scale prints. Half of the fabrics are a variety of light-, medium- and dark-toned yellows and mustards, and the other half are magenta, pink, lilac, aqua, teal, sage, lime, royal blue, light blue, rust, caramel, purple and chocolate.

Materials

44–45in (112cm) wide 100% cotton fabrics:
• *Patch fabrics:* scraps of fabrics in the colours outlined in the *Colour Recipe*
Plus, for the table runner only:
• *Backing fabric:* 1yd (1m)
• *Outer-binding fabric:* $^1/_2$ yd (45cm) of a mustard and dark red two-colour stripe

ABOVE The Crazy Squares Cushion and Table Runner against my painting showing the detail of knitted fabric that inspired the design.

• Cotton batting, at least 3in (7.5cm) larger all around than finished pieced table runner
Plus, for the cushion cover only:
• *Backing fabric:* $^1/_2$ yd (45cm)
• 16in (41cm) cushion pad (pillow form)
• Matching sewing thread
• 14in (35cm) zipper (optional)

Patch shapes

The patchwork is made from four different square blocks that are all the same size. The blocks are made up of fabric strips sewn together using the simple foundation-piecing method. The finished blocks measure 4in x 4in (10cm x 10cm).

BLOCK ASSEMBLY

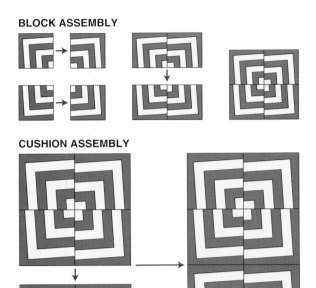

CUSHION ASSEMBLY

Foundation papers

The four foundation papers (A, B, C and D) used for this quilt are on page 156 (see pages 146 and 147 for foundation-piecing instructions). Before beginning the patchwork, make a total of 80 copies of block-A, block-B, block-C and block-D foundation papers for the table runner, or a total of 16 copies for the cushion cover using a random number of each block.

Cutting strips for square blocks

Cut the fabric into $1^{1}/_{2}$ in (4cm) wide strips of any length. These strips are used to piece the blocks.

Making the blocks

Using the paper foundations and following the instructions for paper piecing on pages 146 and 147, make the blocks. Use two colours in each block, making a yellow or a mustard one of the two colours in most

of the blocks. Occasionally make a 'mistake' by using the wrong colour in one or two places in the block.

For the table runner, make a total of 80 blocks; for the cushion cover 16 blocks.

Assembling

When assembling the patchwork, use the seam allowance marked on the foundation paper throughout. Following the diagram, arrange the blocks in groups of four so that all of the smallest patch pieces (patch no. 1) are placed in the centre. (Note that the stripes do not match at the seams.)

Arranging the various foundation-pieced blocks at random, make 20 four-piece blocks for the table runner, or four four-piece blocks for the cushion cover.

For the table runner, join the four-piece blocks together in two rows of 10 blocks, then join the two rows together.

For the cushion cover, join the four-piece blocks together in two rows of two blocks, then join the two rows together.

Finishing the table runner and cushion

Remove the foundation papers and press the assembled patchwork table runner top or cushion cover front.

For the table runner, layer the patchwork top, batting and backing, and baste (see page 147). Quilt in-the-ditch around each of the foundation-pieced blocks. Trim the edge. Cut the binding strips on the bias and attach (see page 148).

For the cushion cover, with right sides facing, stitch the backing to the patchwork, either leaving an opening for inserting the cushion or inserting a zipper in one seam. Turn the cover right side out and insert the cushion pad (pillow form). Stitch the opening closed or simply close the zipper.

Super Triangles Baby Quilt

One of my first big successes in knitting patterns was a jacket design called Super Triangle. Featured on the cover of Woman and Home magazine in London in the 80s, the knitting kit was a run away success, selling 7,000 in a month. The interesting thing about this design is that the knitting was inspired by an antique Irish quilt (see page 8), then the knitting in its turn was the source for this jaunty Super Triangles Quilt.

The colours of the Super Triangles are glowing but never raw or over-bright, the whites never brilliant and always broken with plaids or stripes. The entire patchwork is made up of stripes and plaids with the exception of one leafy green fabric. Along with the glowing deep pastels there is a minky brown that tempers the rest of the palette, keeping it from getting too fresh. The sharp triangles give enough life! The two striped borders and binding are the fabrics I designed to be woven in India.

Size of quilt

The finished patchwork quilt measures 34in x 52in (86cm x 132cm). *Note that the quilting will slightly reduce the final measurements.*

Colour recipe

The fabrics used for the strips of triangles in the quilt centre are mostly mini-plaids, stripes, and some small-scale monochromatic prints. The colours for the quilt centre are separated into lights and darks. The *darks* are plums, denim blue, burgundy, reds, magenta and purples. The *lights* are yellows, pinks, beiges, pumpkins, peach, baby blue, greys and sage greens.

The inner triangle-strip border (border no. 1) is mostly dark magentas and reds, and light greens and beiges. The outer triangle-strip border (border no. 3) is mostly dark blues and purples, and light pinks and yellows.

The two other borders (border nos. 2 and 4) are cut from the same multi-coloured, warm-toned striped fabric.

The border corner-squares are buttercup yellow and navy.

Materials

44–45in (112cm) wide 100% cotton fabrics:
• *Light fabrics:* scraps in the light colours outlined in the *Colour Recipe*
• *Dark fabrics:* scraps in the dark colours outlined in the *Colour Recipe*
• *Borders nos. 2 and no. 4:* $1\frac{1}{2}$yd (1.4m) of a multi-coloured, warm-toned stripe
• *Border corners:* scraps of buttercup yellow and navy fabric
• *Backing fabric:* $1\frac{3}{4}$yd (1.6m)
• *Outer-binding fabric:* $\frac{1}{2}$yd (45cm) of a striped fabric
Plus the following materials:
• Cotton batting, at least 3in (7.5cm) larger all around than finished pieced quilt top
• Cotton quilting thread

Patch shapes

The quilt centre (and part of the border) is made from four sizes of triangles that are sewn together in strips using the simple foundation-piecing method. The finished strips measure 9in x $3\frac{1}{2}$in (24cm x 9cm), 9in x $2\frac{1}{2}$in (24cm x 6cm), 9in x $1\frac{3}{4}$in

RIGHT The Super Triangles Baby Quilt showing its versatility as a table cover.

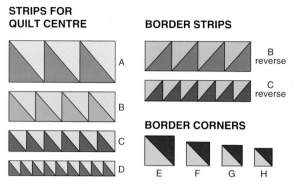

STRIPS FOR QUILT CENTRE

A

B

C

D

BORDER STRIPS

B reverse

C reverse

BORDER CORNERS

E F G H

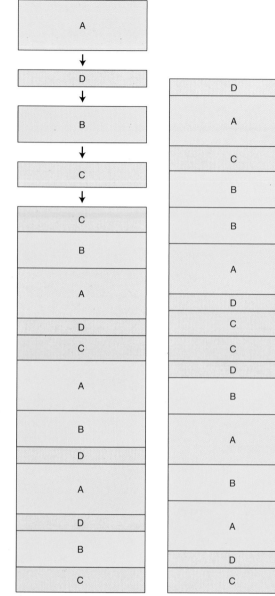

JOINING CENTRE PANELS

(24cm x 4.5cm), and 9in x 1¼in (24cm x 3cm). The only other patch shape used is the right-angled triangle used for the border corner squares.

Foundation papers

The four foundation-paper strips (A, B, C and D) used for this quilt are given on page 151 (see pages 146 and 147 for foundation-piecing instructions). Before beginning the quilt, make the required number of copies of each foundation strip.

Strip-A, B, C and D foundation papers: 8 copies each.

Strip-B-reverse foundation paper: 12 copies.

Strip-C-reverse foundation paper: 16 copies.

SPECIAL NOTE The 'reverse' strips are used for the borders. To make strip-B reverse and strip-C reverse, trace strips B and C on tracing paper, turn the tracing over and redraw the lines on the wrong side of the paper. Then renumber the triangles from right to left. For the reverse foundation strips, copy the reversed image that is on the wrong side of the tracing paper.

Cutting pieces for quilt centre

When making blocks using the paper-foundation-piecing technique, it is not necessary to cut exact patches. The patches can be cut in very rough shapes as the strips are stitched (see page 146).

Cutting pieces for border strips

Borders nos. 1 and 3: cut the patches for these paper-foundation-pieced borders as the strips are stitched using the colours in the *Colour Recipe*.

Border no. 2: from the bold striped fabric, cut two strips measuring 2½in x 23½in (6.5cm x 59.5cm) and two strips measuring 2½in x 41½in (6.5cm x 105.5cm), cutting so that the stripes run across the strips widthways.

JOINING BORDERS

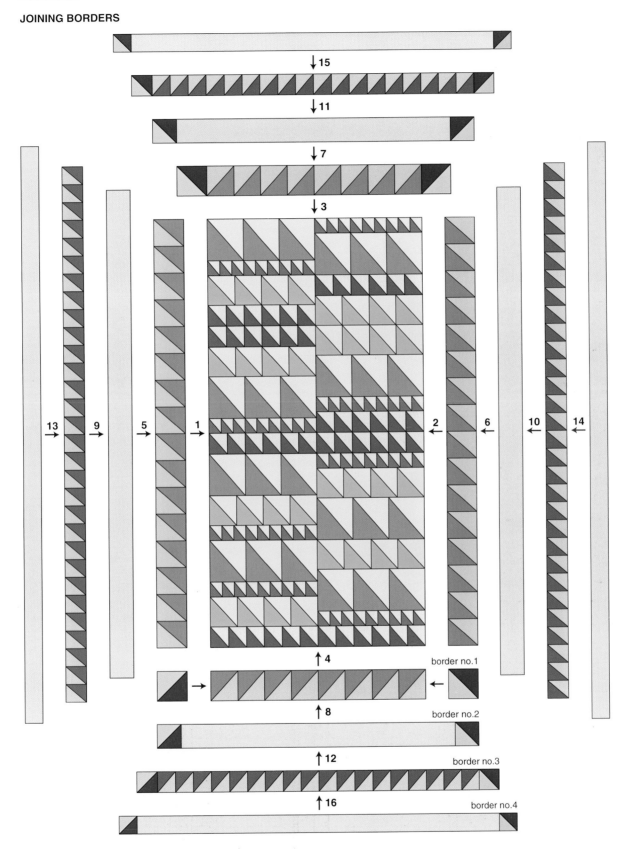

Border no. 4: from the striped border fabric, cut two strips measuring 2in x 31in (5cm x 79cm) and two 2in x 49in (5cm x 124.5cm),

cutting so that the stripes run widthways. SPECIAL NOTE All cutting sizes include the seam allowances.

ABOVE The Super Triangles design uses the paper–foundation–piecing technique.

Cutting pieces for border corners

Corner E: cut two navy and two yellow squares each measuring $3\frac{3}{8}$in x $3\frac{3}{8}$in (8.5cm x 8.5cm), then cut the squares in half diagonally to make a total of four navy triangles and four yellow.

Corner F: cut two navy and two yellow squares each measuring $2\frac{7}{8}$in x $2\frac{7}{8}$in (7.5cm x 7.5cm), then cut the squares in half diagonally to make a total of four navy triangles and four yellow.

Corner G: cut two navy and two yellow squares each measuring $2\frac{5}{8}$in x $2\frac{5}{8}$in (6.5cm x 6.5cm), then cut the squares in half diagonally to make a total of four navy triangles and four yellow.

Corner H: cut two navy and two yellow squares each measuring $2\frac{3}{8}$in x $2\frac{3}{8}$in (6cm x 6cm), then cut the squares in half diagonally to make a total of four navy triangles and four yellow.

SPECIAL NOTE All cutting sizes include the seam allowances.

Making the centre strips

Using the foundation papers and using light-fabric pieces in the odd-numbered areas and dark-fabric pieces in the even-numbered areas, make 8 A-strips, 8 B-strips, 8 C-strips and 8 D-strips for the quilt centre following the instructions for foundation piecing that are given on pages 146 and 147.

Assembling the quilt centre

When assembling the quilt, use the seam allowance marked on the foundation pieces throughout. Following the diagram, arrange the triangle strips in two panels of 16 strips, with the dark triangles all pointing upwards. Join the strips in each panel, then join the two panels together.

Making the border strips

Using the paper foundations and using light-fabric pieces in the odd-numbered areas and dark-fabric pieces in the even-numbered areas, make 12 B-reverse strips and 16 C-reverse strips (see *Colour Recipe*).

For border no. 1, join two B-reverse strips twice for the top and bottom borders and four B-reverse strips twice for the side borders as shown in the diagram, making sure that the dark triangles all point in same direction on each strip. For border no. 3, join three C-reverse strips twice for the top and bottom borders, and five C-reverse strips twice for the side borders, again making sure that the triangles all point in the same direction on each strip.

Join one yellow triangle to one navy triangle for each of the 16 border-corners. Join the corners to the ends of the top and bottom strips of each of the four borders, positioning so that the dark triangles will all be pointing outwards.

Joining the borders

Following the diagram, join the long pieces of border no. 1 to the sides of the quilt centre with the dark triangles all pointing outwards. Then sew on the top and bottom of border no. 1. Continue in this way joining on the sides of each border first, then the top and bottom until all four borders have been joined on.

Finishing the quilt

Remove the foundation papers and press the quilt top. Layer the quilt top, batting and backing, and baste together (see page 147). Quilt in-the-ditch around each of the strips in the quilt centre and in the seams between the borders. Trim the quilt edge. Then attach the binding (see page 148).

Circus Tents Wall Hanging

What is it about bold stripes that get more and more important as I get on in life? They are magnetic, particularly when in many variations of contrast and tone like they are in the Circus Tents Wall Hanging. These bold tents, echoing all the beach tents, marquees and circuses of my childhood, inspired a knitted throw and a knitted Tents waistcoat for my Rowan Yarn *California Patches* knit collection.

The two versions of Tents are made using different techniques, the Burgundy version on page 123 employs a simpler technique.

Size of wall hanging

The finished Circus Tents Wall Hanging measures 48½ in x 68½ in (123cm x 174cm). The Burgundy Tents version is the same size. *Note that the quilting will slightly reduce the final measurements.*

Circus Tents colour recipe

Half of the fabrics for the 'tents' (fabric A) is a *light group* including hot ochres, aqua, pale pinks, pumpkin and rusty orange; the other half is a *dark group* in maroons, dull plums, medium blues, teal, malachite, leaf greens, magenta, rusts and lavenders. The colours used for the 'sky' are greys, grey-blues and lavender-greys (fabric B). Small-scale monochromatic prints and solid-coloured fabrics are used for both A and B.

The borders are cut from fabric B – lavender-greys for the inner border and dull plums and medium blues for the outer.

Alternative colour recipe

Burgundy Tents (page 123): The fabrics used for the 'tents' are a variety of multi-coloured stripe patterns in blues, ochres, lavenders, reds and olives (fabric A). The fabrics used for the 'sky' are mostly solid-coloured with a few small-scale mono-chromatic prints, and the colour range includes burgundy, maroon, blackcurrant, rust and dark red (fabric B).

The inner border is in the same tones as the 'sky' and the outer border is a multi-coloured stripe with a blue cast.

Materials

44–45in (112cm) wide 100% cotton fabrics:
Circus Tents version
• *Fabric A:* ⅛yd (15cm) or more each of at least 8 different fabrics in the colours outlined in the *Colour Recipe*
• *Fabric B:* ⅛yd (15cm) or more each of at least 5 different fabrics in the colours outlined in the *Colour Recipe*
• *Backing fabric:* 2½yd (2.3m)
• *Outer-binding fabric:* ½yd (45cm) of a multi-coloured stripe
Burgundy Tents version
• *Fabric A:* ⅛yd (15cm) or more each of at least 8 different striped fabrics in the colours outlined in the *Colour Recipe*
• *Fabric B:* ⅛yd (15cm) or more each of at least 5 different fabrics in the colours out-lined in the *Colour Recipe*
• *Outer-border and outer-binding fabrics:* ¾yd (70cm) of a multi-coloured stripe with a blue cast
• *Backing fabric:* 2½yd (2.3m)

RIGHT I designed the Pieced Stripes Quilt to echo the stripes on the Circus Tent Wall Hanging. The knitted blanket was taken from the Tents waistcoat I made for the Rowan Yarn *California Patches* book.

Both versions

- Cotton batting, at least 3in (7.5cm) larger all around than finished pieced patchwork
- Cotton quilting thread

Patch shapes

The two versions of the Tents wall hanging are made using two different techniques. The Circus Tents version is made from two different square blocks that are the same size. Both blocks are made using the simple foundation-piecing method. One block (T) – the base of the 'tent'– is made up of fabric strips sewn together. The other block (S) – the top of the 'tent' and the 'sky' – is made up of fabric strips and triangles sewn together.

The Burgundy Tents version is made using templates. The base of the 'tent' is made from a simple square patch (template Z) cut from a bold striped fabric. The top of the 'tent' and the 'sky' is a square block made from two sizes of triangles (templates X and Y), with the 'tent' triangle cut from a bold striped fabric.

The finished squares on both the Circus Tents and Burgundy Tents versions measure 5in x 5in (12.5cm x 12.5cm).

Foundation papers and templates

The two foundation papers (S and T) used for the Circus Tents version are given on page 149 and the instructions for foundation piecing are given on pages 146 and 147. Before beginning the patchwork, make 48 copies each of block-S and block-T foundation papers.

The three templates (X, Y and Z) for the Burgundy Tents version are given on page 149. Note that template Z (the large square) should be drawn using template Y (the half square).

Above Detail of the Circus Tents patchwork. See page 123 for the Burgundy Tents version.

Cutting

Follow the instructions for one version. SPECIAL NOTE All cutting sizes and templates include the seam allowance.

'TENT' BLOCK ASSEMBLY FOR CIRCUS TENTS

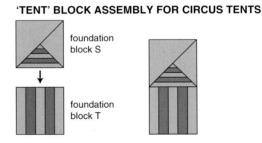

foundation block S

foundation block T

TEMPLATES FOR BURGUNDY TENTS

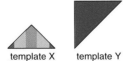

template X   template Y   template Z

'TENT' BLOCK ASSEMBLY FOR BURGUNDY TENTS

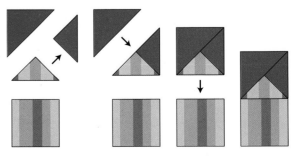

QUILT ASSEMBLY FOR CIRCUS TENTS

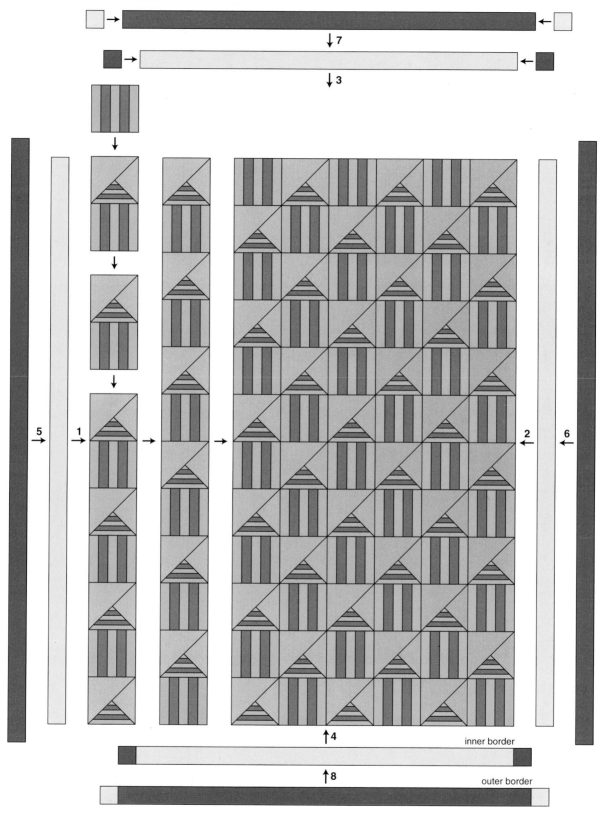

inner border

outer border

Circus Tents version

'*Tent' areas:* cut some 2in (5cm) wide strips of any length from fabric A, cutting more

as the foundation-paper blocks are pieced.

'*Sky' areas:* cut some squares measuring about $6\frac{1}{2}$ in x $6\frac{1}{2}$ in (16.5cm x 16.5cm) from fabric B, cutting more as the foundation-paper blocks are pieced.

Inner border: cut random lengths of $2^{1}/_{2}$ in (6.5cm) wide strips from the lavender-greys for a total of at least $6^{1}/_{4}$ yd (5.7m) in length; cut four $2^{1}/_{2}$ in (6.5cm) squares from the maroons and dull plums.

Outer border: cut random lengths of $2^{1}/_{2}$ in (6.5cm) wide strips from the dull plums and medium blues for a total of at least 7yd (6.4m) in length; cut four $2^{1}/_{2}$ in (6.5cm) squares from the lavender-greys.

Burgundy Tents version

'Tent' patches: cut 48 template-Z squares from fabric A for the 'tent' bottoms and 48 template-X triangles from fabric A for the 'tent' tops, cutting in pairs so that the top and bottom of each tent is cut from the same striped fabric and so that the stripes run perpendicular to the base of the triangle. (Note that the stripes on the 'tent' tops and bottoms will not match at the seam.)

'Sky' patches: cut 48 template-X triangles and 48 template-Y triangles from fabric B for the 'sky', cutting in matching pairs so that there are sets of one large and one small triangle in the same fabric.

Inner border: cut random lengths of $2^{1}/_{2}$ in (6.5cm) wide strips from fabric B for a total of at least $6^{1}/_{4}$ yd (5.7m) in length; cut four $2^{1}/_{2}$ in (6.5cm) squares from the ochre coloured stripes.

Outer border: from the outer-border fabric, cut two strips $2^{1}/_{2}$ in x $44^{1}/_{2}$ in (6.5cm x 113cm) and two strips $2^{1}/_{2}$ in x $64^{1}/_{2}$ in (6.5cm x 164cm), cutting so that the stripes run across the strip widthways; cut four $2^{1}/_{2}$ in (6.5cm) squares from a fabric B.

Making the blocks

Follow the instructions for the Circus Tents or the Burgundy Tents as desired.

Circus Tents version

Using the foundation papers, make the blocks (see pages 146 and 147). Using two colours of fabric A for each, make 48 T-blocks for the 'tent' bottoms.

Using two colours of fabric A for each 'tent' top and a single fabric B for each 'sky', make 48 S-blocks. Occasionally make 'mistakes' in the 'tent' stripes by using a maverick colour for a stripe.

Using the seam allowance marked on the foundation pieces throughout, sew 44 S-blocks to the top of matching T-blocks to make 44 'tents' as shown in the diagram given on page 58, leaving 4 S-blocks and 4 T-blocks unattached.

Burgundy Tents version

Select a template-X triangle and a template-Y triangle cut from the same fabric B for the 'sky', then select a template-X triangle and a template-Z square cut from the same fabric A for the 'tent'.

Using the seam allowance marked on the templates throughout, join the fabric-A and fabric-B small template-X triangles together as shown in the diagram given on page 58. Then sew these joined triangles to the large template-Y triangle to complete the block for the sky and 'tent' top. Make a total of 48 blocks in this way.

Sew 44 'tent'-top blocks to the top of matching template-Z striped squares to make 44 'tents', leaving 4 'tent'-top blocks and 4 template-Z 'tent'-bottom squares unattached.

Assembling the patchwork centre

For both versions of the patchwork, follow the diagram given on page 59 and arrange the tents in rows.

Join the tents together in vertical rows, then join the rows together.

Making the inner border

Join together end-to-end the $2^1/2$ in (6.5cm) wide strips that were cut for the inner border. Then cut from the joined strips, two side border pieces measuring $60^1/2$ in (153.5cm) and a top and bottom piece each measuring $40^1/2$ in (103cm). Sew the border corners to the ends of the top and bottom strips.

Join on the two side borders, then sew on the bottom and top borders.

Making the outer border

For the Circus Tents version only, join together end-to-end the $2^1/2$ in (6.5cm) wide strips that were cut for the outer border. Then cut from the joined strips, two side border pieces measuring $64^1/2$ in (164cm) and a top and bottom piece each measuring $44^1/2$ in (113cm).

For both versions, join the border corners to the ends of the top and bottom strips. Join on the two side borders, then sew on the bottom and top borders.

Finishing the wall hanging

Press the assembled patchwork (first removing foundation papers on the Circus version). Layer the patchwork top, batting and backing and baste (see page 147).

For the Circus Tents version, quilt in-the-ditch between the strips in the 'tent' bottom and continue these lines to form spokes that converge at the point of the 'tent' top using a rust-coloured quilting thread. Quilt cloud-shaped swirls in the sky with a grey quilting thread.

For the Burgundy Tents version, quilt five equally spaced vertical lines in the 'tent' bottom and continue these lines to form spokes that converge at the point of the 'tent' top using pumpkin-coloured

QUILTING FOR BURGUNDY TENTS VERSION

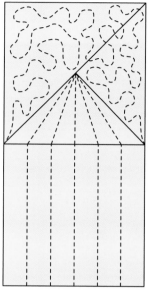

quilting thread. Quilt cloud-shaped swirls in the sky with dark red quilting thread.

For both versions, trim the quilt edge and attach the binding (see page 148).

Pieced Stripes Quilt

The bold stripes of the Pieced Stripes Quilt would make a great quilted coat. Actually, the idea for the patchwork design was taken from a Japanese kimono made of scraps of brocades in long stripes. What I did here was to take the colours of my Circus Tents Wall Hanging and scale them up on a bedcover. The way the close tones melt together to create a rich stripe could be repeated in a simpler design for a starker, more minimal interior; for instance in off-white and pale greys for a restful effect.

Size of quilt

The finished patchwork quilt measures 85in x 85in (213cm x 213cm). *Note that the metric quilt size will not exactly match the imperial size and that the quilting will slightly reduce the final measurements.*

QUILT ASSEMBLY

Key

▨	fabric-A colour group
▨	fabric-B colour group
▨	fabric-C colour group

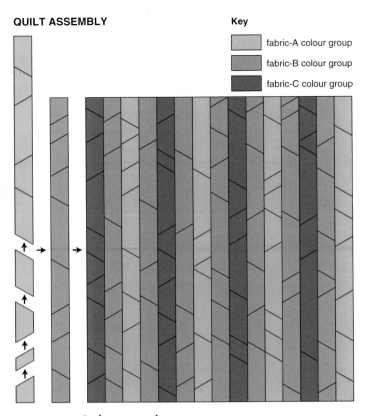

Colour recipe

This scheme has three colour groups. The first colour group is medium shades of moss greens, burnt oranges and ochre-golds (fabric A). The second is shades of medium grey-blues and grey-lavenders (fabric B). The third is shades of brick, magenta, purple and dull rust (fabric C). All the fabrics are small-scale monochromatic prints.

Materials

44–45in (112cm) wide 100% cotton fabrics:
• *Fabric A:* 1/4 yd (25cm) each of at least 15 different prints in the colours outlined in the *Colour Recipe*
• *Fabric B:* 1/2 yd (45cm) each of at least 15 different prints in the colours outlined in the *Colour Recipe*
• *Fabric C:* 1/4 yd (25cm) each of at least 15 different prints in the colours outlined in the *Colour Recipe*
• *Backing fabric:* 6yd (5.5m)

• *Outer-binding fabric:* 3/4 yd (70cm) of a striped fabric
Plus the following materials:
• Cotton batting, at least 3in (7.5cm) larger all around than finished pieced quilt top
• Grey-blue cotton quilting thread

Patch shapes

The quilt top is made from wide strips of fabric of random lengths cut at a 60-degree angle at each end and stitched together end-to-end to form stripes. The finished stripes measure 5in (12.5cm) wide. No templates are needed.

Cutting

Fabric A: cut the fabrics into 5 1/2 in (14cm) wide strips, cutting parallel to the selvedge; then, cutting the ends at a 60-degree angle in either direction (see diagram), cut the strips into random lengths until there is a total of approximately 13 1/2 yd (12.5m) of strips.
Fabric B: cut the fabrics into 5 1/2 in (14cm) wide strips as for fabric A until there is a total of approximately 22yd (20m) of strips.
Fabric C: cut the fabrics into 5 1/2 in (14cm) wide strips as for fabric A until there is a total of approximately 11yd (10m) of strips.
SPECIAL NOTE The cutting sizes include the seam allowance.

Assembling the strips

When assembling the quilt, use a 1/4 in (7.5mm) seam allowance throughout. Following the diagram, arrange the strips into five fabric-A stripes, eight fabric-B stripes and four fabric-C stripes, each at least 90in (226cm) long (taking the seam allowances into account). Matching the angles, join the strips together in stripes 90in (226cm) long. Then trim each of the

ABOVE The Pieced Stripes Quilt makes a bold statement and could be done in any number of different colour combinations.

17 strips to 85in (213cm) long. Join the stripes together as shown in the diagram.

Finishing the quilt

Press the assembled quilt top. Layer the quilt top, batting and backing, and baste together (see page 147). Quilt large uneven zigzags down each stripe (see diagram). Trim the quilt edge and attach the binding (see page 148).

QUILTING

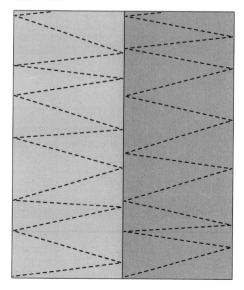

Leafy gardens

I have often gone on in previous books and lectures about the thrill of leaves and about their never-ending variation, stretching from delicate ferns to massive bold banana trees, from gazillion shades of green to deepest magentas and brilliant lavenders. But what especially springs to mind lately is the sheer trembling joy of a leafy glade on a summer day. Little bits of green fluttering in a breeze and catching the sunlight in a field of simple grasses — how deeply beautiful such a scene is when we stop to take it in.

Of course, spring is the most magical time to zero in on leaves if you live in a part of the world where there are real winters. Before flowers upstage the greenery, you can experience those amazing, odd colourings of emerging foliage — the wine pinks and rusty maroons slowly turning to green that give spring woods such a plummy glow.

FACING PAGE One of my favourite American paintings Flowers and Fruit (1850-55) by Severin Roesen (top left and bottom right) is echoed in my Leafy Rosy Quilt (top right) and the Red Diamonds Quilt (bottom left). Instructions for Leafy Rosy and Red Diamonds are given on pages 68–71 and 76–81.

ABOVE The Tawny Rosy Quilt (see page 68 for instructions). RIGHT Tawny Rosy with two needle-point cushions – California Grapes and Ribbon and Rose. The wall was collaged with wallpapers in the same geometric layout as the quilt.

When planning the decoration of the Kaffe Fassett Designs shop in Bath, I could not get the idea of green trees out of my head. Imagining a soft haze of grey-green trees disappearing into the mist, I had the shop painted top to bottom with a neutral sage green, then painted murals of fields and groups of trees and bushes in muddy greens over all the flat surfaces. With decorative mirrors, paintings or plates on this mural, it looks for all the world like an old tapestry.

Every few months I redecorate the upstairs room at the shop and one theme, was a leafy garden. I painted furniture with leaves, flowers and fruit, hung my Apple and Cabbage needlepoint carpet, did a series of fruit and leaf still-lifes, and hooked a rug of autumn leaves in rags. The centre piece was a mosaic garden table of the huge flamboyant cabbage that is painted on the sign outside the shop at 3 Saville Road, Bath.

Many of the pots and dishes I collect feature leaves. I can understand why medieval and Renaissance interiors were crammed with tapestries and murals of tree-filled landscapes; the shades of green that exist in any group of trees have a subtle richness that is infinitely comforting to live with day after day. Ripening vegetables, fruits and flowers enrich and highlight this greenness. With this theme we can bring gardens into the cosiness of our homes.

I could go on and on designing patchworks based on leafy gardens. It was delicious to go from the dense saturated greens of Leafy Rosy (see page 69) to the delicate laciness of Salad Days (see page 72).

My Stamps and Money Quilt (see page 83) may seem the odd man out in this chapter of leafiness until you think of cacti and succulents. The grey-greens and the blushes of lavender and rose on these desert plants create a wonderfully restrained palette. I started the quilt with the idea of old stamps and etched patterns on documents and money in mind, and once it was finished it had a soft garden effect.

As if leaves weren't incredible enough, there is also the fragile intensity of flowers – from the purest white through the deepest vibrant colours. Because flowers are one of the most eternal textile designs, there is no shortage of floral prints for patchworkers to work with.

The Pastel Rosy Quilt (see page 18) was my first attempt at dealing with the new

vocabulary of fabric prints. With it, I was trying to recreate a linen patchwork of old faded roses that I'd slept under when I first came to England in the early 60s. It was hard to find the same quality of old rose prints on the American market, but eventually I did find find some. The finished patchwork left me wanting stronger, more saturated tones, so I am saving painterly, old-fashioned rose prints for my ideal fandango of roses.

If you really want particular flowers in specific tones and moods, it is worth collecting floral prints over a period of time. I have been amassing fabrics with roses for my gypsy rose quilt. Several of my quilts feature roses, but none have achieved the deep intensity of the embroidered Spanish and Chinese shawls that I have seen in museums and antique shops.

The layout of 9-patch and large squares of the Rosy Quilt was an excellent vehicle for other colour schemes. The best one was created by Liza's friend Meg who went for warm, tawny tones. Toasty golds, cinammons, rust roses make a very liveable palette for this Tawny Rosy version (above). Every time I see someone choose an autumn palette or play with those toasty colours myself, I experience all over again how rich and moving the colours are at the end of the year. Some people find autumn sad, but I am too preoccupied by the golden rust, lavender-edged beauty around every corner to feel any regrets. Meg definitely captures that mellow richness in Tawny Rosy.

You can see on pages 18 and 19, where the three versions of Rosy are lined up, how different the same patchwork structure can look if the colours and prints are varied.

Leafy Rosy Quilt

Anyone who knows my work will have spotted my passion for all things leafy. Vegetables and fruits are so enhanced by their framework of greenery. With Leafy Rosy I wanted to create a quilt that would cover a table with lush greenness, much as those Dutch tapestries did when thrown over a table in the old paintings.

A set of dishes made to look like leaves and fruits set on top of the quilt would create a rare banquet that could be topped off with piles of real fruit and vegetables.

There is a strong apple fabric in the border with a very dark ground. This was used for a large square in the original version, but it shouted out too much, so was replaced (patiently by Liza) with a softer leafy pattern. It is one of life's great satisfactions to replace a maverick element in a patchwork that is distracting from the total look. If this discordance is caused by too light a ground on a patch, you can avoid unpicking by applying tea dye with a brush.

Size of quilt

The finished patchwork quilt measures 69in x 78in (184cm x 208cm). *Note that the metric size will not exactly match the imperial size and that the tying or quilting will slightly reduce the final measurements.*

Leafy Rosy colour recipe

This scheme has lots of leafy green prints. The large-scale prints (fabric A) are predominantly green-toned fruits, vegetables and leaves with with a smattering of reds, purples and pinks. The small-scale prints

(fabric B) are the accent fabrics with fruits, vegetables and flowers in greens, teals, deep blue, rust, red and gold. The 'neutral' fabrics (fabric C) are stripes and mini-plaids in greens and green-on-green prints.

This version of the Rosy patchwork was quilted with a stipple-quilt pattern.

Alternative colour recipes

Tawny Rosy (pages 66 and 67): This scheme has the feel of autumn. The large-scale prints (fabric A) are florals with faded antique tones – grey-blue, cinammon, rusty red, gold, plum, olive and forest green. The small-scale patterns (fabric B) are tiny prints and woven mini-plaids in the same tones. The two-tone 'toile' prints (fabric C) have a tea-dyed or beige background with blue, green, maroon or olive figures. This version of the Rosy quilt was tied in the spots indicated on the diagram.

Pastel Rosy (page 18): The overall effect of this scheme is dusty faded floweriness. The large-scale florals (fabric A) are sweet pink, dusty, soft duck-egg and sky blue, pale ochre, mauve, sage, muddy lavender, pale chestnut, dull moss green and rose tones. The small-scale prints (fabric B) have simple design repeats in two or three colours. The two-tone 'toile' prints (fabric C) have faded red, blue, green or brown floral motifs and light, off-white backgrounds. This version of the Rosy quilt was tied in the spots indicated on the diagram.

Materials

44–45in (112cm) wide 100% cotton fabrics:
• *Fabric A:* ¹/₂ yd (45cm) or more each of at least 10 different large-scale prints

RIGHT What a joy to find such a perfect home for the Leafy Rosy Quilt in this English apple orchard.

ABOVE The Leafy Rosy Quilt. See pages 18 and 19 for the two other Rosy colour schemes.

- *Fabric B:* ¼ yd (25cm) or more each of at least 10 different small-scale prints
- *Fabric C:* ¼ yd (25cm) or more each of at least 10 different two-tone 'toile' prints or 'neutral' prints
- *Backing fabric:* 4½ yd (4.2m)
- *Outer-binding fabric:* ½ yd (45cm) of one of the small-scale prints (fabric B)

Plus the following materials:
- Extra fluffy polyester or wool batting suitable for tying (if quilting, use cotton batting), at least 3in (7.5cm) larger all around than finished pieced quilt top
- One ball of 100% wool yarn for tying, or a matching cotton quilting thread
- 86 assorted buttons to embellish the tying (optional)

Patch shapes

The entire quilt is made from only three sizes of square patches. The finished patches measure 9in (24cm) square, 4½ in (12cm) square and 3in (8cm) square.

Cutting

Fabric A: cut 21 large squares 9½ in x 9½ in (25.5cm x 25.5cm); cut 28 medium-sized squares 5in x 5in (13.5cm x 13.5cm); cut 152 small squares 3½ in x 3½ in (9.5cm x 9.5cm).

Fabric B: cut 131 small squares 3½ in x 3½ in (9.5cm x 9.5cm).

Fabric C: cut 28 medium-sized squares 5in x 5in (13.5cm x 13.5cm).

SPECIAL NOTE The cutting sizes include the seam allowance.

Making the blocks

Select four patches the same of the small squares of fabric B and five patches the same of the small squares of fabric A. Using a ¼ in (7.5mm) seam allowance through-out, make a nine-patch block, joining as shown opposite. Make a total of 21 blocks.

Assembling the blocks

Arrange the 21 blocks and the 21 large squares of fabric A into 7 rows. Join the patches in rows, then join the rows.

Making the border

Following the diagram, make the four inner-border strips with the medium-sized squares of fabrics A and C, joining an A square and a C square alternately. Join the strips to the centre panel.

Make the four outer-border strips with the small squares of fabrics A and B, joining an A square and a B square alter-nately. Join these four strips to the side, bottom and top borders.

Finishing the quilt

Press the assembled quilt top. Layer the quilt top, batting and backing, and baste together (see page 147).

BLOCK ASSEMBLY

JOINING ROWS

JOINING BORDERS

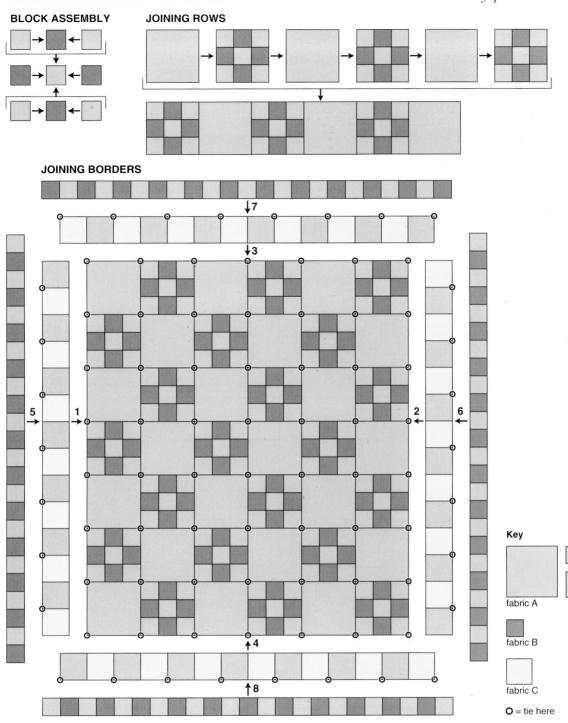

Key

fabric A

fabric B

fabric C

O = tie here

For quilting, stipple quilt as shown in the diagram. For tying, tie through at the spots indicated on the chart, using a 10in (25cm) length of yarn (see page 148 for instructions on tying quilts). If desired, embellish each tie with a button. Trim ends of yarn. Then trim the quilt edge and attach the binding (see page 148).

QUILTING

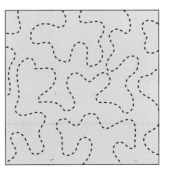

Salad Days

The Salad Days Table Cover was inspired by a set of china that I designed for my shop, Kaffe Fassett Designs in Bath, England. The china, called Cottage Garden, is dappled with a patchwork of vegetable and leafy prints in soft greens. I picked all the soft leafy little prints that I could find with light grounds to create an airy base for my china.

There are many good leafy wallpaper patterns on the market. Wouldn't it be fun to do a collage of these on the walls of your dining room to keep the theme going? A rag rug of little green leaves on creamy pastel tones would be an added richness. You can never have too many leaves!

Size of table cover

The finished table cover measures $60\frac{1}{2}$ in x $72\frac{1}{2}$ in (151.5cm x 181.5cm). *Note that the metric size will not exactly match the imperial size and that the quilting will slightly reduce the final measurements.*

Colour recipe

The fabrics in this colour scheme resemble the kind of prints found on flowery old-fashioned tea sets. The colours are mostly pinks, greens and soft blues with a smattering of yellows and corals.

Materials

44–45in (112cm) wide 100% cotton fabrics:
• *Patch fabrics:* $\frac{1}{4}$ yd (25cm) of at least 30 different medium- and small-scale floral prints (see *Colour Recipe* above)
• *Backing fabric:* 3yd (3m)

LEFT The Salad Days Table Cover. ABOVE RIGHT Salad Days with the cottage garden patchwork china I designed for my shop in Bath.

• *Outer-binding fabric:* $\frac{1}{2}$ yd (45cm) of pink-and-white striped fabric
Plus the following materials:
• Cotton batting, at least 3in (7.5cm) larger all around than finished pieced patchwork
• Light blue cotton quilting thread

Patch shapes

The entire patchwork is made from only one size of square patch. The finished patch measures 3in (7.5cm) square.

Cutting

From the floral patch fabrics, cut 60 sets of 8 matching squares each measuring $3\frac{1}{2}$ in x $3\frac{1}{2}$ in (9cm x 9cm). This makes a total of 480 squares.

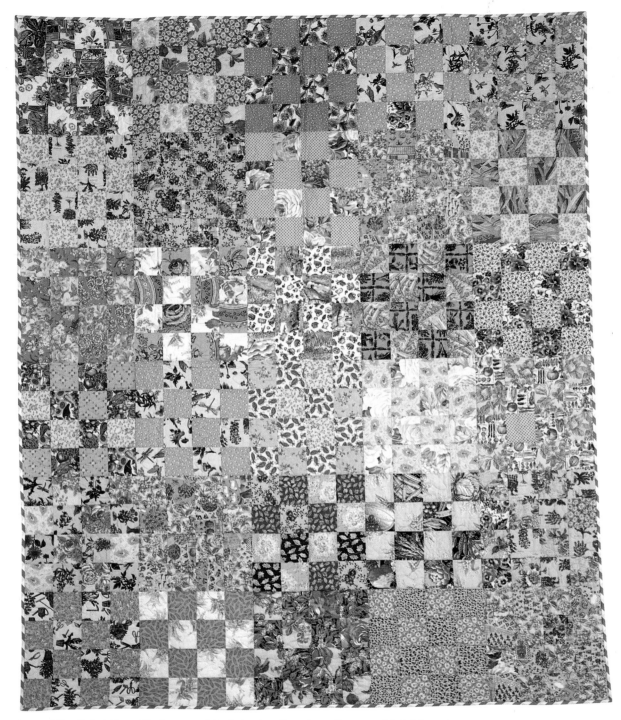

ABOVE The Salad Days fabrics resemble the prints found on flowery old–fashioned tea sets.

Making the blocks and assembling

Select 8 squares each of two fabrics and arrange in a block four patches by four. Using a $\frac{1}{4}$ in (7.5mm) seam throughout, join as shown. Make a total of 30 16-patch blocks, making most of the blocks using a set of green fabrics with a set of pink.

BLOCK ASSEMBLY

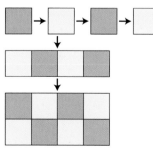

QUILT ASSEMBLY

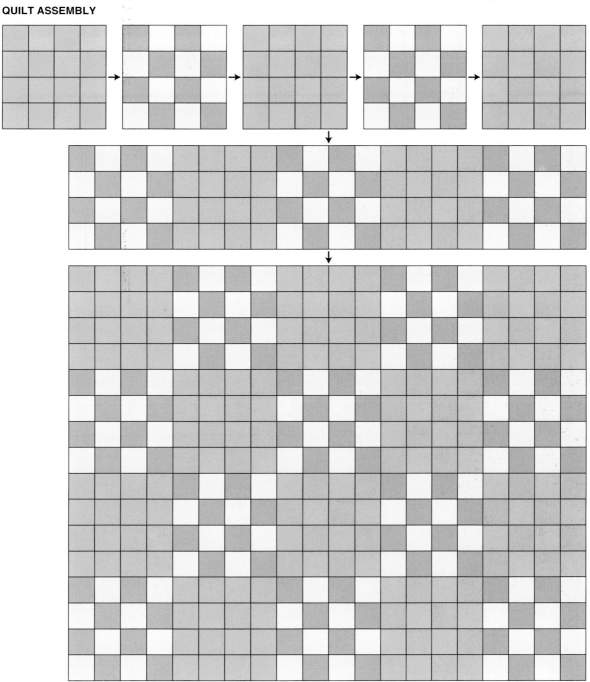

Arrange the blocks in 6 rows of 5 blocks. Join the blocks together in rows, then join the rows together.

Finishing the table cover

Press the assembled patchwork. Layer the patchwork top, batting and backing, and baste together (see page 147). Stipple quilt each block as shown. Trim the quilt edge and attach the binding (see page 148).

QUILTING

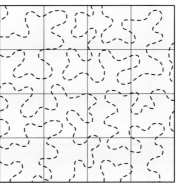

Red Diamonds Quilt

When I published my seventh book, *Glorious Interiors*, I collaged a folding screen of paper flower prints and used a photograph of it as end papers for the book. Cutting flower prints into diamond shapes and slotting them together is a thrilling experience. When you zero in on the centre of large sunflowers or roses and then contrast them with a spray of small blossoms all in vivid colours, it really makes the blood rush!

The screen was an ideal starting point for the Red Diamonds Quilt. The addition of fruit prints to the floral theme added to the voluptuous denseness. If I were to start again on this red quilt, I'd use more fabrics with solid red grounds and more dispersed flower patterns so that the overall red impact would be greater.

The Pinafore-print Diamonds is the same patchwork design, but in cool pastel lavender pinks and pale blues (see pages 14 and 15). The most unusual version is the Striped Diamonds Quilt (see page 120); the positioning of the striped fabrics creates the appearance of squares, and one almost loses any sense of the underlying geometric diamond structure.

Size of quilt

The finished Red Diamonds Quilt measures $92^3/4$ in x $108^1/2$ in (235.5cm x 275.5cm). The Pinafore-print Diamonds version measures 57in x $81^1/2$ in (145cm x 207cm). *Note that the quilting will slightly reduce the final measurements.*

Red Diamonds colour recipe

The diamond patches in the centre of the Red Diamonds quilt are cut from medium- and large-scale floral and fruit prints in

reds, hot pinks, golds, black, sandstone, caramel brown, plums and greens.

The inner diamond border fabric is a medium-scale caramel-brown floral print. The outer border fabric is a glowing pink-and-red stripe.

SPECIAL NOTE Try to cut the floral and fruit prints so that a flower or fruit is centred in each patch.

Alternative colour recipe

Pinafore-print Diamonds (see pages 14 and 15): This colour scheme is based on the kind of fabrics found in old aprons and house dresses and has a nostalgic softness. The diamond patches in the quilt centre are cut from medium- and large-scale floral prints in a range of blues (duck egg, grey-blue and turquoise), lavenders and pinks.

The inner diamond border is a large-scale floral print in pink on sage, the outer border a narrow blue-and-white stripe.

Materials

44–45in (112cm) wide 100% cotton fabrics:
Red Diamonds version
• *Main-diamonds fabrics:* $^3/4$ yd (70cm) each of 21 different medium- and large-scale floral and fruit prints
• *Inner-border fabric:* $1^1/2$ yd (1.4m) of a medium-scale floral print
• *Outer-border fabric:* $^3/4$ yd (70cm) of a striped fabric
• *Backing fabric:* $6^1/2$ yd (6m)
• *Outer-binding fabric:* $^3/4$ yd (70cm) of the same striped fabric as the outer border
Pinafore-print Diamonds version
• *Main-diamonds fabrics:* $^3/4$ yd (70cm) each of 15 different medium- and large-scale floral and fruit prints
• *Inner border fabric:* $1^1/2$ yd (1.4m) of a medium-scale floral print

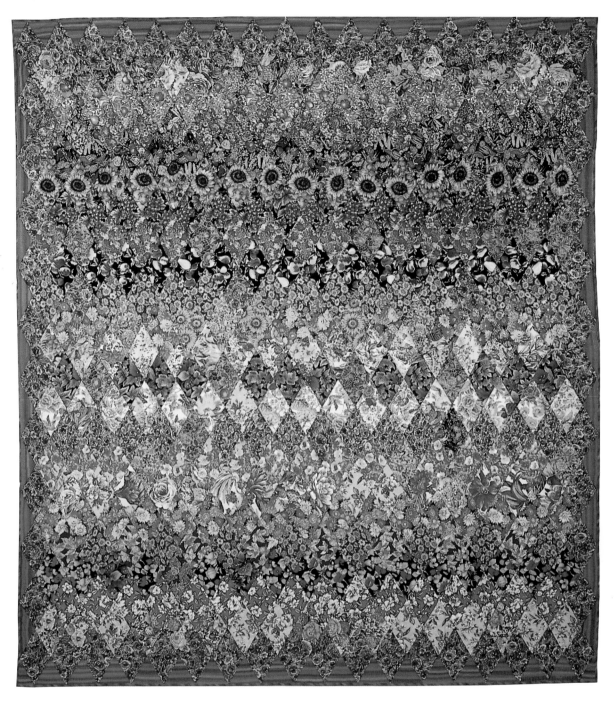

ABOVE AND OVERLEAF Using fruit prints with the flowers helps build up the voluptuous denseness of the Red Diamonds patchwork.

- *Outer-border fabric:* ³⁄₄yd (70cm) of a stripe
- *Backing fabric:* 4yd (3.7m)
- *Outer-binding fabric:* ³⁄₄yd (70cm) of the same striped fabric as the outer border

Both versions

- Cotton batting, at least 3in (7.5cm) larger all around than finished pieced quilt top

- Dark red cotton quilting thread for Red Diamonds; pink for Pinafore-print

Patch shapes

The centre of the quilt is made from a single diamond shape (template A). The border is made from 3 patch shapes –

ASSEMBLY FOR RED DIAMONDS QUILT

TEMPLATES

template A   template B   template C   templates D
and D reverse

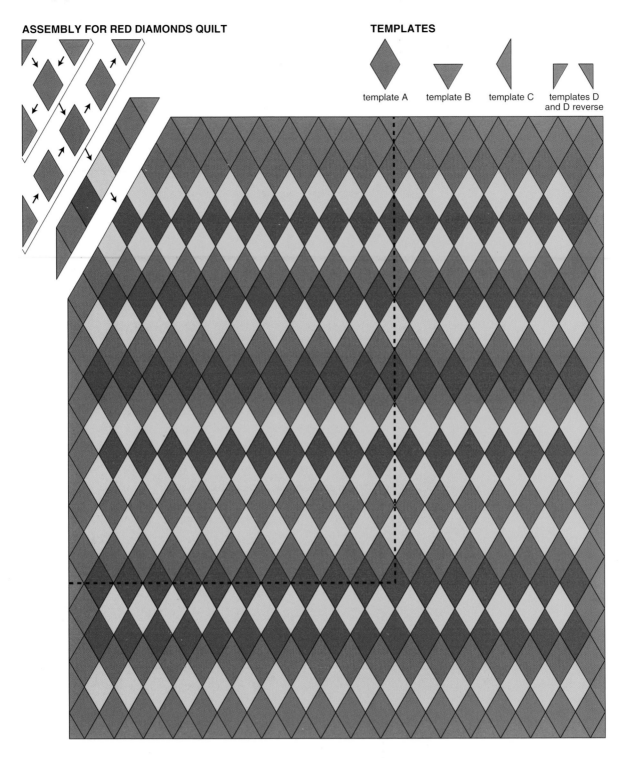

two half diamonds (templates B and C), and a quarter diamond (template D) and a reverse–quarter diamond (template D reverse). The actual-size templates for the quilt are given on page 150. Trace and make templates as explained in Patchwork Basics on page 144.

Cutting

The quilts are different sizes. Follow the cutting instructions for your chosen version.

Red Diamonds version

Template A for centre quilt: cut 18 diamonds each from 21 different floral prints (this will allow a few extra diamond patches to use as 'mistake' diamonds in the rows).

Template A for inner border: cut 56 diamonds from the inner-border fabric.

Template B: cut 34 from the outer-border striped fabric, cutting so that the stripe runs parallel to the base of the triangle.

Template C: cut 20 from the outer-border striped fabric, cutting so that the stripe runs parallel to the base of the triangle.

Template D and D reverse: cut 2 each from the outer-border striped fabric, cutting so that the stripe runs parallel to the short side of the triangle.

Pinafore-print Diamonds version

Template A for centre quilt: cut 11 diamonds each from 15 different floral prints (this will allow a few extra diamond patches to use as 'mistake' diamonds).

Template A for inner border: cut 36 diamonds from the inner-border fabric.

Template B: cut 20 from the outer-border striped fabric, cutting so that the stripe runs parallel to the base of the triangle.

Template C: cut 16 from the outer-border striped fabric, cutting so that the stripe runs parallel to the base of the triangle.

Template D and D reverse: cut 2 each from the outer-border striped fabric, cutting so that the stripe runs parallel to the short side of the triangle.

Arranging the patches

The Red Diamonds and Pinafore-print Diamonds are not the same size, so the arrangement is not exactly the same; the instructions for the Red Diamonds are given first and those for the Pinafore-print Diamonds follow in square brackets. (The size of the Pinafore-print version is shown by the broken line on the diagram.)

Following the diagram, arrange the centre of the quilt first. Take 17 [10]

diamonds cut from the same fabric and arrange them in a horizontal row. Then take 16 [9] diamonds cut from the same fabric and arrange them in the next horizontal row. Continue in this way, arranging horizontal rows of the same fabric, alternating the 17- [10-] diamond rows and the 16- [9-] diamond rows, until there are 21 [15] rows. Place an occasional 'mistake' diamond in a row.

Arrange 18 [11] inner-border diamonds along the top of the quilt and 18 [11] along the bottom, then arrange 10 [7] inner-border diamonds along each side.

Arrange the outer border around the outer edge, using the template-B, template-C and template-D patches.

Assembling the patches

When assembling the quilt, use the seam allowance marked on the templates throughout. Following the diagram, sew the patches together in diagonal rows, taking special care to remember the border patches at the end of each row. Join the diagonal rows together.

Finishing the quilt

Press the assembled quilt top. Layer the quilt top, batting and backing, and baste together (see page 147).

Quilt the Red Diamonds version with stitch-in-the-ditch quilting using a dark red quilting thread. Using a pink quilting thread, quilt the Pinafore-print Diamonds version with outline quilting by stitching $\frac{1}{4}$ in (6mm) from each seam line (see the quilting diagram on page 29 for an example of outline quilting on diamond patches.)

Trim the quilt edge. Then cut the binding on the bias from the striped binding fabric and attach (see page 148).

Stamps and Money Quilt

Getting acquainted with the fabric collections available in American quilting stores, I kept spotting copies of two-colour prints that really had the etched, mellow richness of old stamps and came up with the idea for the Stamps and Money patchwork. The finished quilt has a quality that slowly reveals itself as you live with it. What at first appears to be just a few patterns become more and more complex as you gaze across the multi-coloured composition.

When choosing and arranging these prints the trick is to keep the fabrics all close in value so that none shouts out above the others. The large crazy-patch blocks ('landscape' blocks) were inspired by farm land viewed from the air. The shades of dusty green and earthy tones off odd-shaped farmed fields is very similar in value to printed money.

I enjoyed making the mosaic lamps and stamp-covered lampshades to go in a set for the Stamps and Money Quilt. The collaged wallpaper was made from great ripped chunks of about ten close-toned Designers Guild wallpapers that were glued down with gay abandon. When finished, the collage was given a glaze of green acrylic to neutralize the tones.

To go with the quilt, I knitted a scarf of muted squares in wools and mohair. I get such a bounce from seeing the same theme and coloration in so many contrasting textures and media.

There are those who feel patchwork should always be playing with a dark-light contrast, which I do like. But the melting together of textures in Stamps and Money also appeals to me, in the same way as a marble floor composed of many subtle shades or a marquetry box where all the articulated elements of the design are depicted in a close range of amber browns.

Size of quilt

The finished patchwork quilt measures 92in x 92in (230cm x 230cm). *Note that the metric quilt size will not exactly match the imperial size and that the quilting will slightly reduce the final measurements.*

Colour recipe

This scheme has the lithographic-look of printed money and classic old stamps. The colours are all dusty tones and include muddy roses, sage and moss greens, mint greens, beiges, grey-blues and lavenders.

All of the fabrics are prints with the type of very fine, small-scale details that you find on stamps and money; most are simple prints and fine plaids, and some are two-tone 'toile' prints.

Materials

44–45in (112cm) wide 100% cotton fabrics:
• *Patch fabric:* scraps of many different small-scale prints in the colours outlined in the *Colour Recipe*
• *Outer border no. 1:* $^{1}/_{2}$ yd (45cm) of a fabric with a small-scale print containing many of the colours listed in the *Colour Recipe*
• *Backing fabric:* $6^{1}/_{2}$ yd (6m)
• *Outer-binding fabric:* $^{3}/_{4}$ yd (70cm) of a small-scale granite-green print

RIGHT Collaged wallpaper, stamp lampshades on mosaic vases and a knitted scarf continue the mood of the Stamps and Money Quilt.

Key

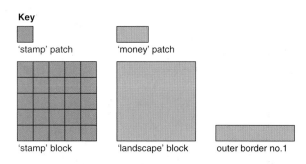

'stamp' patch   'money' patch

'stamp' block   'landscape' block   outer border no.1

Plus the following materials:
• Cotton batting, at least 3in (7.5cm) larger all around than finished pieced quilt top
• Beige cotton quilting thread

Patch shapes

Most of the quilt is made from two patches – the 'stamp' square, which measures 2in x 2in (5cm x 5cm) when finished, and the 'money' rectangle, which measures 2in x 4in (5cm x 10cm) when finished.

The centre medallion of the quilt is made from the 'stamp' patches. All three inner borders and two of the outer borders are made from the 'money' patches.

Two types of blocks are arranged around the centre medallion – one of these is made of stamp patches, and one is made of random patches and is called a 'land-scape' block.

CENTRE MEDALLION ASSEMBLY

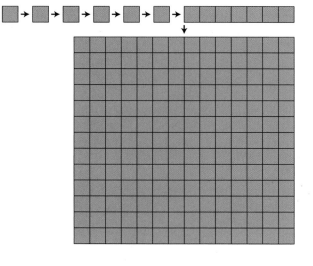

Cutting

'Stamp' patches: cut 800 squares $2\frac{1}{2}$in x $2\frac{1}{2}$in (6.5cm x 6.5cm) from the full range of colours in the *Colour Recipe* given on page 82.

'Money' patches: cut 278 rectangles $2\frac{1}{2}$in x $4\frac{1}{2}$in (6.5cm x 11.5cm) from the full range of colours in the *Colour Recipe*.

'Landscape' block fabric: cut many long lengths of $2\frac{1}{2}$in–4in (6.5cm–10cm) wide strips in a variety of greens and beiges (see *Special Note* below).

Outer border no. 1: cut 4 strips $2\frac{1}{2}$in x $80\frac{1}{2}$in (6.5cm x 201.5cm) from a single small-scale print containing many of the colours listed in the *Colour Recipe*.

SPECIAL NOTE All cutting sizes include the seam allowance. The random-shaped 'landscape'-block patches are cut from the strips as the blocks are stitched.

Making the centre medallion

Arrange 196 'stamp' patches in assorted colours into a block 14 'stamps' by 14 'stamps'. When assembling the patches, use a $\frac{1}{4}$in (7.5mm) seam allowance through-out. Join the patches together in rows, then join the rows together.

Making the 'stamp' blocks

Arrange 25 'stamp' patches in assorted colours into a square five 'stamps' by five 'stamps'. Join the patches together in rows, then join the rows together. Make a total of 24 'stamp' blocks.

Making the 'landscape' blocks

The finished patches on the 'landscape' block should be random, free-form shapes. Each block should be different. Begin the block by selecting a group of about 9 or 10 'landscape' strips.

LANDSCAPE-BLOCK ASSEMBLY

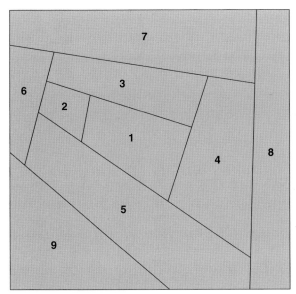

When making the block, use a $\frac{1}{4}$in (7.5mm) seam allowance throughout and follow the landscape-block assembly diagram shown above as a rough guide. To begin, cut a piece of fabric from one of the strips into a 4-sided patch measuring 2in–4in (5–10cm) on each side, cutting it into a trapezoid (or a parallelogram) shape for the centre (patch 1). With patch 1 right side up, place another piece of fabric (patch 2) face down on patch 1 and line up the patches along one edge (the edges will not be the same length). Sew the patches together along this edge. Open out the joined patches so that they are both right side up. With patch 2 at the top, ★trim the right-side edge to straighten it. With the joined patches still right side up, place another piece of fabric (patch 3) face down on the joined patches and line it up with the edge just trimmed. Sew in place along this edge. Open so that the joined patches are all right side up. With patch 3 at the top, repeat from ★, adding another new piece along the trimmed edge until the total block is bigger than $10\frac{1}{2}$in (26.5cm) square. Press the block, then trim

ABOVE Old marbled book covers, money and stamps on the Stamps and Money Quilt.

to $10\frac{1}{2}$in (26.5cm) square. Make a total of 24 'landscape' blocks in this way.

Making the 'money' borders

Sewing the 'money' patches together end-to-end, make two strips 7 patches long, four strips 8 patches long, four strips 9 patches long, two strips 10 patches long, two strips 21 patches long, four strips 22 patches long and two strips 23 patches long.

JOINING INNER BORDERS

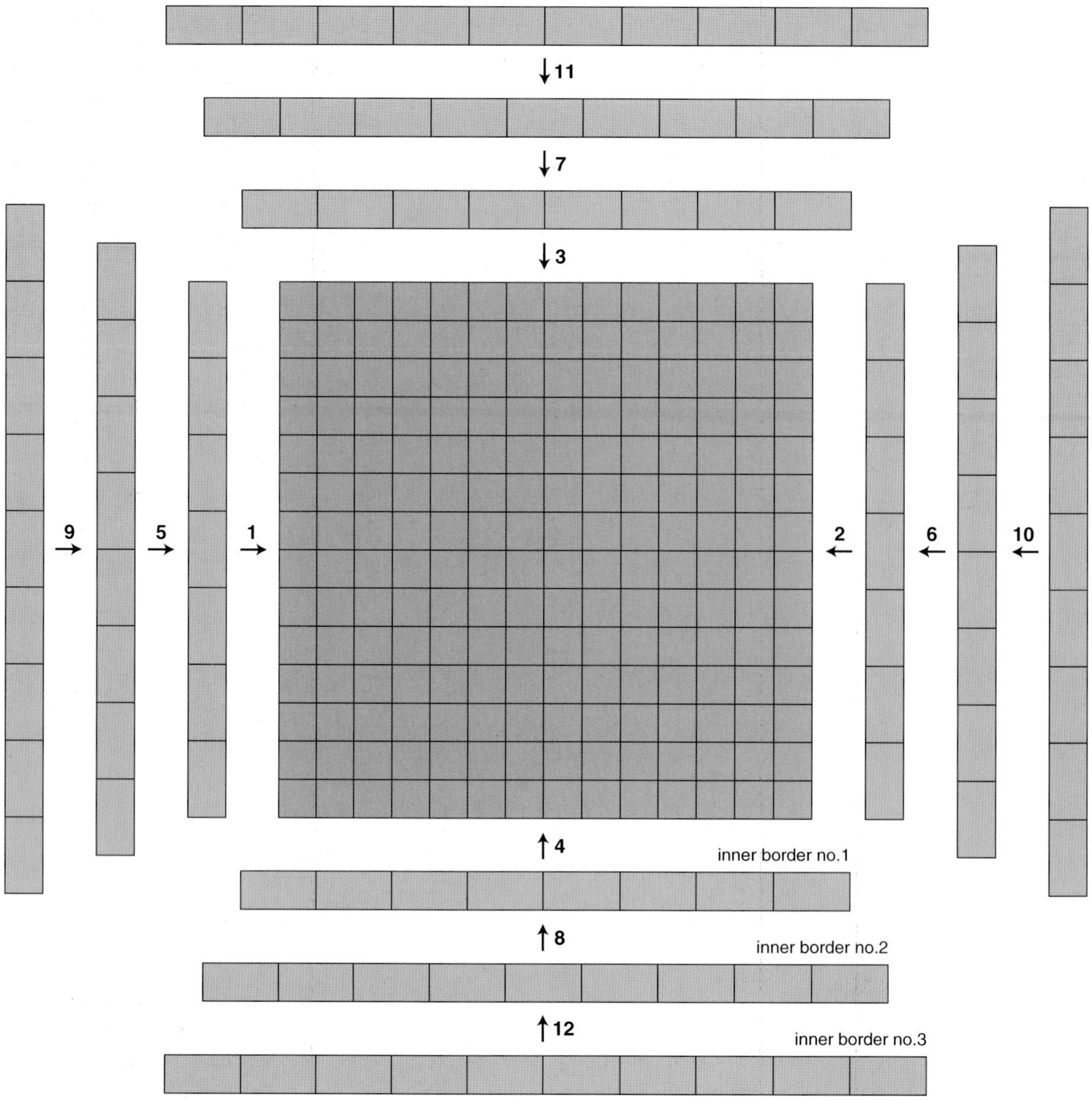

inner border no.1

inner border no.2

inner border no.3

Assembling the inner borders

Following the diagram shown above, sew inner border no. 1 to the centre medallion by joining a 7-patch 'money' strip to each side, then an 8-patch 'money' strip each to the top and bottom.

Join the remaining two inner borders (border no. 2 and border no. 3) in the same way, using two 8-patch and two 9-patch 'money' strips for border no. 2, and two 9-patch and two 10-patch 'money' strips for border no. 3.

Assembling the blocks

Following the diagram shown on the opposite page, arrange the 'stamp' blocks and the 'landscape' blocks around the centre medallion so that they alternate.

As shown on the diagram, join the blocks in two rows of four blocks for each side, then join the rows to the centre medallion.

Join the blocks in two rows of 8 blocks for the top and bottom, then join them to the centre medallion.

ABOVE The Stamps and Money Quilt was inspired by old stamps and money.

JOINING BLOCKS

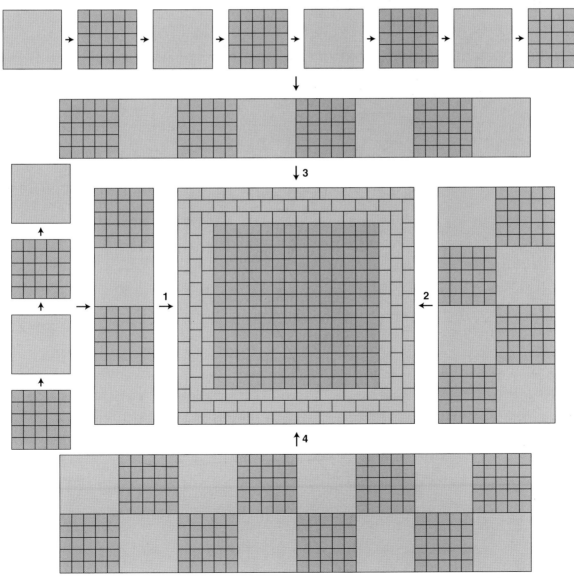

JOINING OUTER BORDERS

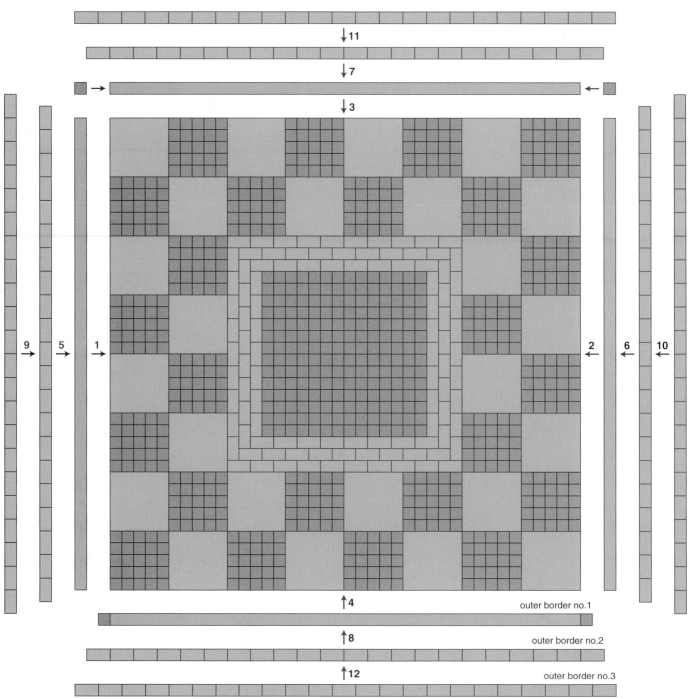

↓11

↓7

→ ←

↓3

9→ 5→ 1→ 2← 6← 10←

↑4   outer border no.1

↑8   outer border no.2

↑12   outer border no.3

LANDSCAPE-BLOCK QUILTING

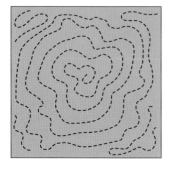

STAMP-PATCH QUILTING

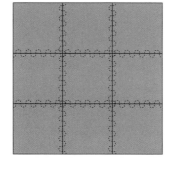

MONEY-BORDER QUILTING

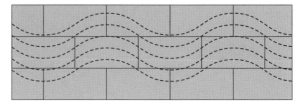

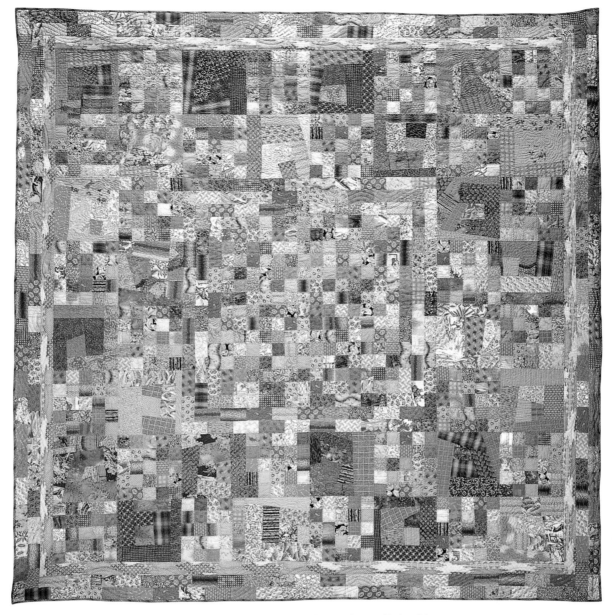

ABOVE When choosing and arranging the prints the trick is to keep all the fabrics
very close in value so that none shouts out above the other.

Assembling the outer borders

Following the diagram, sew two strips of
outer border no. 1 (the solid-fabric border)
to the sides of the quilt. Sew a 'stamp'
patch to each end of the two remaining
strips and then sew these to the top and
bottom of the quilt. Join the remaining
two outer borders in the same way, using
two 21-patch and two 22-patch 'money'
strips for border no. 2, and two 22-patch
and two 23-patch 'money' strips for no. 3.

Finishing the quilt

Press the quilt top. Layer the top, batting
and backing, and baste (see page 147).
Quilt concentric wavy lines $1/2$ in (1.5cm)
apart along the 'money'-patch borders, and
wiggly lines that look like stamp perfora-
tions over the seam lines on the 'stamp'
patches. On the 'landscape' blocks, quilt
concentric wavy lines in a circle like the
lines on topographical maps. Trim the edge
and attach the binding (see page 148).

Antique stone

For years I started colour lectures with 'When I first got to England from California, I had to come to terms with grey'. Actually, it was a very positive experience to find that these supposed monotones had such endless variations. Firstly, I noticed that the grey skies and soft defused light made colours glow rather than appear washed out like they can in sharp California light. Then gradually I began to be aware of subtle silver and bronze garden tones and, best of all, discovered the intense beauty of stone. A range of chalky pinks, greens, blues, browns and ochres became visible to me in those so-called grey stones, as seen in the warm camel shades of Bath stone in the west of England and the cool green blues of the Lake District cliffs in the north. The red bricks too were suddenly alive to my colour eye. And the 'yellow' brick buildings, which had at first appeared mostly ochre grey, slowly revealed mysterious shades of smoky blues, lavenders, plums and golds.

FACING PAGE A pebble mirror frame by Candace Bahouth and stones from Budley Salterton (top left) set the mood for this stony chapter. The Marble Venetian Tile Quilt at the Mercer Museum (top right), inspired by the mosaic floor at St Mark's in Venice (bottom left), and the Taupe Lattice Quilt (bottom right) illustrate the effective use of quiet colour schemes in patchwork.

A chapter based on stone colours in a book on colour furnishings isn't as strange as it might sound. One only need visualize the thrilling range of colours in those handsome stone walls in Scotland – pale pinks, greens, grey blues, warm plum tones, deep granite, blacks and peaty browns.

After composing the subtle numbers in this chapter – Floating Blocks, Taupe Lattice and Venetian Tiles – I also explored the deeper tones of Navy Bricks, a dark lapis sort of look, and the bright rose quartz feel of Pink Roman Blocks. The Navy Bricks Quilt (right) has two distinct influences – African strip-weaving, which supplied the idea for the layout for these brick shapes, and Fonthill (see right), which inspired its texture and colour.

Henry Mercer, whose home Fonthill is now preserved as a museum, was as obsessive a collector as I am, and he made brilliant use of treasures in his everyday life. He had a passion for tiles and pottery, and collected and made wonderful tiles with which he studded his house. Fonthill is one of the first precast concrete structures and its Byzantine interior sports columns, domes, arches and a labyrinth of corridors and odd staircases. Every interior surface is encrusted with earthy coloured tiles, paintings or shelves of old leather books.

Mercer was undoubtedly drawn like I am to cultures that revel in tiled walls of ceramic patchwork. Many of his own rather medieval, yet unique, creations are three-dimensional shapes that look for all the world like edible gingerbread. Having realized his vision with laudable thoroughness, Henry Mercer should be an inspiration to anyone attempting to create their own look. I urge you to visit the lovingly preserved Fonthill 'castle' and Mercer Museum in Doylestown, Pennsylvania.

The multi-coloured striped fabrics used in the Navy Bricks were designs I did for the Oxfam International charity. On my first trip to India, in 1993, I heard about Oxfam's work with craftsmen and women all over India and thought how exciting it would be to help create fabrics in the rich colours of old Indian miniatures.

When a year later Oxfam offered me the job of putting my ideas to work, I jumped at the chance and started by knitting a series of stripes of different widths – always with gobs of luscious Indian colours.

When I arrived at the weaving village, I was disappointed to find out that the woven samples hadn't even been started. The colours I had chosen were not available in cotton of the right weight. With only just over a week to spare, I was anxious to get on, so we drove for eight hours to the nearest store with the right yarns. There I completely redesigned my stripes under awful strip lighting in the cotton-dying house.

We then returned to the weavers and spent the next few days stretching out the multi-coloured warp down the main street of the village. Five different stripes were put on the same piece, involving more than 50 colours. The result was a collection that has not only been exciting to work with on my own quilt designs, but has been used creatively by fellow quilters, giving a small village the chance of a livelihood.

RIGHT The Navy Bricks Quilt in the sympathetic interior of Fonthill in Doylestown, Pennsylvania. (See page 21 for quilt instructions.)

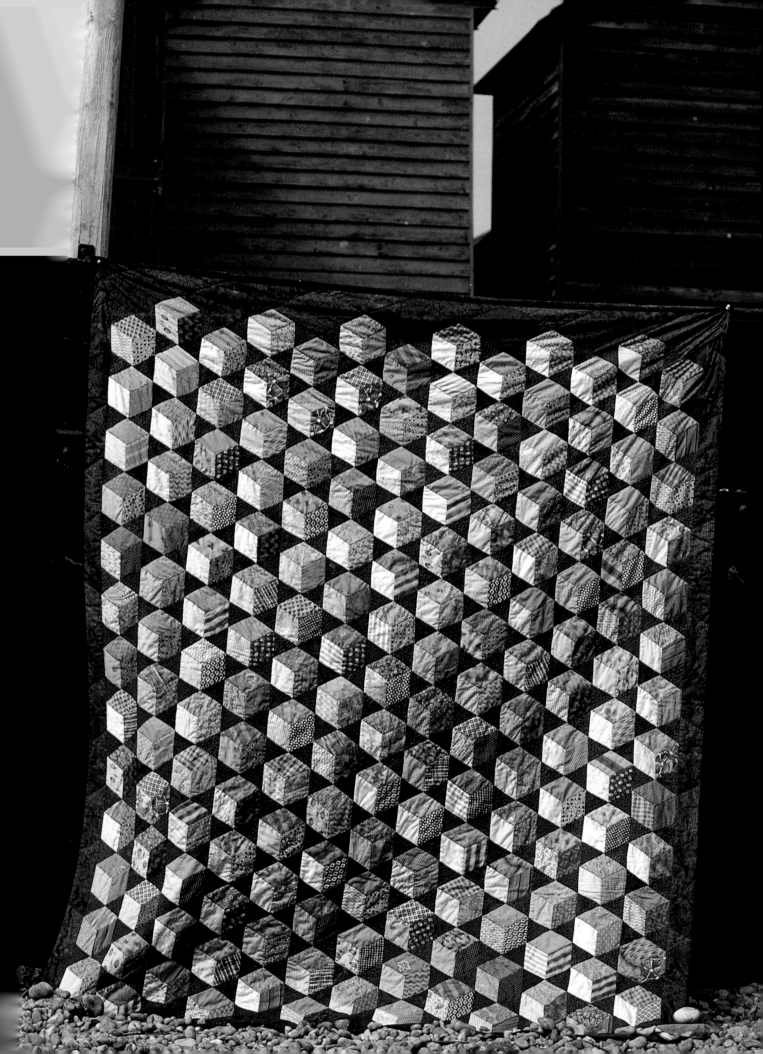

Tweed Floating Blocks

For years I have played with the classic tumbling blocks as a knitting pattern, but this floating variation, spotted in an old patchwork book, looked quite fresh. It's amazing how different the subtle browns and beiges on a black ground look compared with the pale blue version of the design on page 16.

As with the Stamps and Money Quilt (see page 83), the cube tones on the Tweed Floating Blocks have been kept quite close, even though dark, light and medium tones are needed to create the illusion of cubes. Only muddy wine tones and dirty blue liven up the beige-brown greyness of the restrained palette.

One of the great joys of having had so large a selection of fabrics to choose from in the American patchwork shops was that we could lay hands on dozens of almost black variants. A backdrop of peat brown on black, midnight navy on black, and so on, made a very rich dark ground for the cubes indeed. I once knitted a version of tumbling blocks in deep maroons, bottle greens and inky navys with black as the shadow side of each box. For a very dramatic dark patchwork you could do the same with close-toned dark brocades.

The Tweed Floating Blocks Quilt was photographed on the coast in the south of England. The tall windowless black houses are designed for drying nets. These long dark shapes on the stony Hastings beach have a medieval presence.

The Jewel Floating Blocks Quilt is a variation of the same geometry, designed

in an alternative colour scheme, with dark punchy jewel tones (see page 120). The third version, the Pale Floating Blocks, has a Scandinavian feel (see page 16).

Size of quilt

The finished Tweed Floating Blocks Quilt measures 74in x 90½in (188cm x 230cm). The Pale Floating Blocks version measures 74in x 72½in (188cm x 184cm) and the Jewel Floating Blocks version measures 74in x 54½in (188cm x 138.5cm). *Note that the quilting will slightly reduce the final measurements.*

Tweed Floating Blocks colour recipe

The fabrics and colours to use are those found in traditional men's clothing and handkerchiefs. The fabrics used for the patchwork 'cubes' are small-scale prints, plaids and stripes that are all mostly monochromatic.

The colours used for the 'cubes' are beiges, steel blues, aquas, mauves, caramel, browns, greys, golds, and sages, all separated into light (fabric A), medium (fabric B) and dark tones (fabric C).

The background fabrics (fabric D) are very dark browns, black and charcoals in monochromatic prints that appear almost solid at a distance.

Alternative colour recipes

Pale Floating Blocks (page 16): The mood for this scheme is a chalky lightness. The fabrics used for the patchwork 'cubes' are small-scale monochromatic prints, and mini-plaids, stripes and checks. The colours

LEFT The subtle tones of the Tweed Floating Blocks Quilt look quite lively against the austere net-drying houses on Hastings Beach.

used for the 'cubes' are peachy pinks, blues, taupes, cool mint greens, sages, fresh whites, off-whites and creams. These colours are all fairly light, but are separated into three tone groups called 'light' (fabric A), 'medium' (fabric B) and 'dark' (fabric C). (The trick with the Pale Floating Blocks colour scheme is to keep it as light as possible.)

The background (fabric D) is a man's shirting stripe in light blue and white. *Jewel Floating Blocks* (page 120): The colour scheme for this version is a range of jewel shades. The three-dimensional effect of the patchwork 'cubes' is very subtle. All the fabrics are small-scale prints, florals and mini-plaids. The colours used for the patchwork 'cubes' are reds, olives, magenta, navy, oranges, brilliant greens, periwinkle, browns and mustards, all separated into light (fabric A), medium (fabric B) and dark tones (fabric C).

The background fabrics (fabric D) have very dark purple, turquoise, green and maroon ground with black prints.

Materials

44–45in (112cm) wide 100% cotton fabrics:
• *Fabric A:* scraps of an assortment of light-toned fabrics
• *Fabric B:* scraps of an assortment of medium- toned fabrics
• *Fabric C:* scraps of an assortment of dark-toned fabrics
• *Fabric D* (background fabric): $^1\!/_2$ yd (45cm) or more of at least 6 different prints for Tweed and Jewel versions, or 3yd (3m) of the background striped fabric for Pale version
• *Backing fabric:* $5^1\!/_4$ yd (4.8m) for Tweed version, $4^1\!/_2$ yd (4m) for Pale version and $3^1\!/_2$ yd (3.2m) for Jewel version
• *Outer binding:* $^3\!/_4$ yd (70cm) of fabric D
Plus the following materials:
• 100% cotton batting or traditional-thickness mixed cotton and polyester batting, at least 3in (7.5cm) larger all around than finished pieced quilt top
• Cotton quilting thread
• One ball of off-white wool yarn for tying, for Pale version only

Patch shapes

The patchwork 'cubes' are made from a single small diamond shape (template S). The patchwork background between the cubes is made from a single small equilateral triangle (template T), and the border background is made from one large diamond shape (template U), three triangles (templates V, V reverse and W) and a trapezoid shape (template X). The actual-size templates are given on page 154.

'CUBE' TEMPLATE

template S

BACKGROUND TEMPLATES

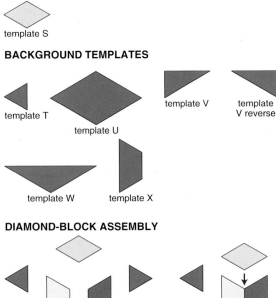

template T

template U

template V   template V reverse

template W   template X

DIAMOND-BLOCK ASSEMBLY

ASSEMBLY FOR TWEED FLOATING BLOCKS

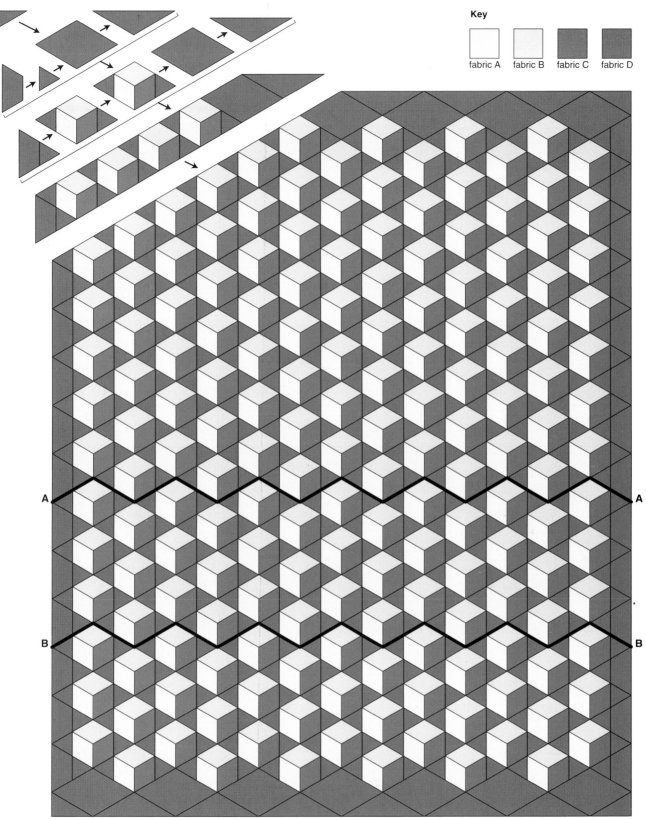

Key

fabric A fabric B fabric C fabric D

Cutting

The three versions of the Floating Blocks
Quilt are different sizes. Follow the cutting
instructions for your chosen version.

Tweed Floating Blocks version

Template S: cut 175 small diamonds each
from fabric A, fabric B and fabric C
(making a total of 525 diamonds).

Template T: cut 378 small equilateral triangles from fabric D.

Template U: cut 14 large diamonds from fabric D.

Template V and V reverse: cut 2 each from fabric D.

Template W: cut 12 from fabric D.

Template X: cut 28 from fabric D.

Pale Floating Blocks version

Template S: cut 136 small diamonds each from fabrics A, B and C (a total of 408).

Template T: cut 294 small equilateral triangles from fabric D, cutting so that the stripes run parallel to the base on some and perpendicular to the base on others.

Template U: cut 14 large diamonds from fabric D, cutting so that the stripes run lengthways down the diamond.

Template V and V reverse: cut 2 each from fabric D, cutting so that the stripes run parallel to the base of the triangle.

Template W: cut 12 from fabric D, cutting so that the stripes run parallel to the base of the triangle.

Template X: cut 22 from fabric D, cutting so that the stripes run parallel to the base of the trapezoid.

Jewel Floating Blocks version

Template S: cut 97 small diamonds each from fabrics A, B and C (a total of 291).

Template T: cut 210 small equilateral triangles from fabric D.

Template U: cut 14 large diamonds from fabric D.

Template V and V reverse: cut 2 each from fabric D.

Template W: cut 12 from fabric D.

Template X: cut 16 from fabric D.

Making the diamond blocks

Select one S-template diamond each in fabrics A, B and C. Arrange these three

diamonds following the block assembly diagram on page 96. Using the seam allowance marked on the templates throughout, sew the two bottom diamond patches together, then stitch the top diamond patch to the two joined patches using a set-in seam (see page 145). Sew a template-T background triangle to each side of the cube (positioning the stripes for the Pale version at random).

Make a total of 175 diamond blocks for the Tweed version, 136 for the Pale version and 97 for the Jewel version.

SPECIAL NOTE The position of the light side of the 'cube' can be either on the right or left side, but should remain consistent throughout the quilt to give the illusion that the 'light source' is coming from a single direction.

Arranging the patches

Following the diagram on page 97, arrange the centre of the quilt. Select 6 diamond blocks and arrange them in a horizontal row. Then take 7 diamond blocks and arrange them in the next horizontal row between the diamonds of the first row.

Continue in this way, arranging horizontal rows with 6 and 7 diamond blocks alternately, until there are a total of 27 rows for the Tweed version, 21 for the Pale version or 15 for the Jewel version. (The 'cubes' go to the bold line AA for the Jewel version and to the bold line BB for the Pale version).

Arrange 7 template-U diamonds and 6 template-W triangles across the top of the quilt and across the bottom of the quilt. Arrange the template-V and template-V reverse triangles in the four corners, then arrange the template-T and template-X patches along the sides of the quilt.

Assembling the patches

Following the diagram, sew the border patches and blocks together in diagonal rows. Join the diagonal rows together.

Finishing the quilt

Press the quilt top. Layer the quilt top, batting and backing, and baste (see page 147).

For the Tweed version, quilt in-the-ditch in the border seams. Then stipple quilt (see page 71) the background triangles.

QUILTING FOR PALE FLOATING BLOCKS

QUILTING FOR JEWEL FLOATING BLOCKS

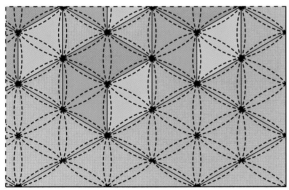

For the Pale version, quilt the background patches with wavy lines as shown above; then tie through the layers at the centre of each 'cube' using a length of yarn.

For the Jewel version, quilt 'petals' in a hexagonal pattern as shown in the diagram, using a dark matching thread for the border and a light contrasting thread for the quilt centre.

For all versions, trim the quilt edge and attach the binding (see page 148).

Pink Roman Blocks Quilt

The source for the patchwork structure of the Pink Roman Blocks Quilt came from a Roman mosaic and the pink cast of it was inspired by pink quartz. I don't know about you, but I feel pink is an invigorating colour. It brings to mind Mexican houses painted inside and out with a strong pink, and decorated with deeper pink, oranges and reds. This quilt would sparkle in a pink room (see page 11).

The original Roman mosaic had a little contrasting square in the centre of each cube. I have used buttons instead as that accent. What fun it was raiding inexpensive end-of-line button collections in yarn stores and flea markets to find those piquant bright touches of colour.

Notice how different the chalky Blue Roman Blocks version looks (see page 37). Basically, I approached both colourways in the same way, taking a pool of blues on the one hand and pinks and reds for this version. Blues and lavenders creep into the hot pinks to cool them down, whereas plums and lavenders give a subtle warmth to the cool blue palette.

Size of quilt

The finished Pink Roman Blocks Quilt measures $60^{1}/_{2}$ in x $72^{1}/_{2}$ in (153.5cm x 184cm). The Blue Roman Blocks version measures $78^{1}/_{2}$ in x $90^{1}/_{2}$ in (199cm x 230cm). *Note that the quilting will slightly reduce the final measurements.*

Pink Roman Blocks colour recipe

The fabrics used in this colour scheme are small-scale multi-coloured and monochromatic prints, and mini-plaids, checks and stripes. The colours used for the patchwork 'cubes' are pink, red, lilac, lavender, tomato, plum, periwinkle and lilac, all separated into three tone groups – light to medium (fabric A), medium (fabric B) and dark (fabric C).

The background colours for the 'cubes' in the quilt centre are an assortment of deep teals, ochres and grey-greens (fabric D). The background colours for the border 'cubes' are an assortment of golden ochres (fabric E).

Buttons in aquas, reds, oranges, blues, lilac, pinks, turquoise and olive are used to highlight the centres of the 'cubes'.

Alternative colour recipe

Blue Roman Blocks (page 37): The fabrics used for the patchwork 'cubes' in this colour scheme are small-scale multi-coloured and monochromatic prints, and mini-plaids. The colours for the 'cubes' used a wide range of blues, purples and plums, all separated into three tone groups – light to medium (fabric A), medium (fabric B) and dark (fabric C).

The background for the 'cubes' in the quilt centre is a solid-coloured taupe fabric (fabric D). The background for the border 'cubes' is a solid-coloured black fabric (fabric E).

Buttons in blues, teals, reds, purples and greens are used to highlight the centres of the 'cubes'.

Materials

44–45in (112cm) wide 100% cotton fabrics:
• *Fabric A:* scraps of an assortment of light-toned to medium-toned fabrics

• *Fabric B:* scraps of an assortment of medium-toned fabrics
• *Fabric C:* scraps of an assortment of dark-toned fabrics
• *Fabric D (background):* for the Pink version, scraps of an assortment of fabrics; for the Blue version, $1^3/4$ yd (1.6m) of a solid-coloured taupe fabric
• *Fabric E (background):* for the Pink version, scraps of an assortment of fabrics; for the Blue version $^3/4$ yd (70cm) of a black fabric
• *Backing fabric:* $3^3/4$ yd (3.5m) for the Pink version, or $5^1/4$ yd (4.8m) for the Blue version
• *Outer-binding fabric:* $^1/2$ yd (45cm) of fabric E
Plus the following materials:
• 100% cotton batting or traditional thickness mixed cotton and polyester batting, at least 3in (7.5cm) larger all around than finished pieced quilt top
• Cotton quilting thread
• 120 buttons in various sizes, shapes and materials for the Pink version, or 195 for the Blue version

Patch shapes

The patchwork 'cubes' are made from three patch shapes – a square (template V) and two mirror-image parallelograms (templates W and W reverse). The patchwork background between the cubes is made from a single small equilateral triangle (template X).

The actual-size templates are given on page 155. (See page 143 for instructions on how to work with templates.)

RIGHT The Pink Roman Blocks Quilt draped over a boat and photographed on Hastings beach on the south coast of Britain.

template V

BACKGROUND TEMPLATE

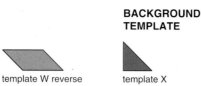

template W   template W reverse   template X

Cutting

The two versions of the Roman Blocks Quilt are different sizes. Follow the cutting instructions for your chosen version using the *Colour Recipe* for the colours for fabrics for A, B, C, D and E.

Pink Roman Blocks version

Template V: cut 120 squares from fabric A.
Template W: cut 120 from fabric B.
Template W reverse: cut 120 from fabric C.
Template X (background): cut 80 pairs of matching triangles from fabric D for background at centre of quilt (a total of 160); and cut 40 pairs of matching triangles from fabric E for background in border blocks (a total of 80).

Blue Roman Blocks version

Template V: cut 195 squares from fabric A.
Template W: cut 195 from fabric B.
Template W reverse: cut 195 from fabric C.
Template X (background): cut 286 triangles from fabric D for background at centre of quilt; and cut 104 triangles from fabric E for background in border blocks.

Making the blocks

Select one V-template square (fabric A), one template-W parallelogram (fabric B), one template-W-reverse parallelogram (fabric C) and two template-X triangles

cut from the same fabric D. Then arrange the patches following the block assembly diagram shown below left. Using the seam allowance marked on the templates throughout, sew the two parallelograms together, then stitch the square patch to the two joined patches using a set-in seam. Lastly, sew the two template-X 'background' triangles to the parallelograms.

For the Pink version, make a total of 120 blocks, 80 with fabric D 'background' patches, and 40 with fabric E 'background' patches.

For the Blue version, make a total of 195 blocks, 143 with fabric D 'background' patches, and 52 with fabric E 'background' patches.

Assembling the quilt

For the Pink version, follow the assembly diagram and arrange the centre of the quilt into 10 horizontal rows of 8 blocks with fabric-D backgrounds.

For the Blue version, arrange the centre of the quilt with 13 horizontal rows of 11 blocks with fabric-D backgrounds.

For both versions, place the blocks with fabric-E backgrounds all around the outside of the quilt to form the border. Join the blocks together in rows, then join the rows together.

QUILTING FOR BLUE VERSION

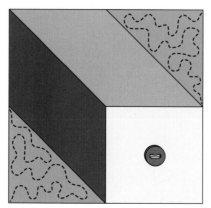

BLOCK ASSEMBLY

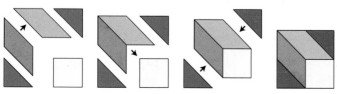

ASSEMBLY FOR PINK ROMAN BLOCKS

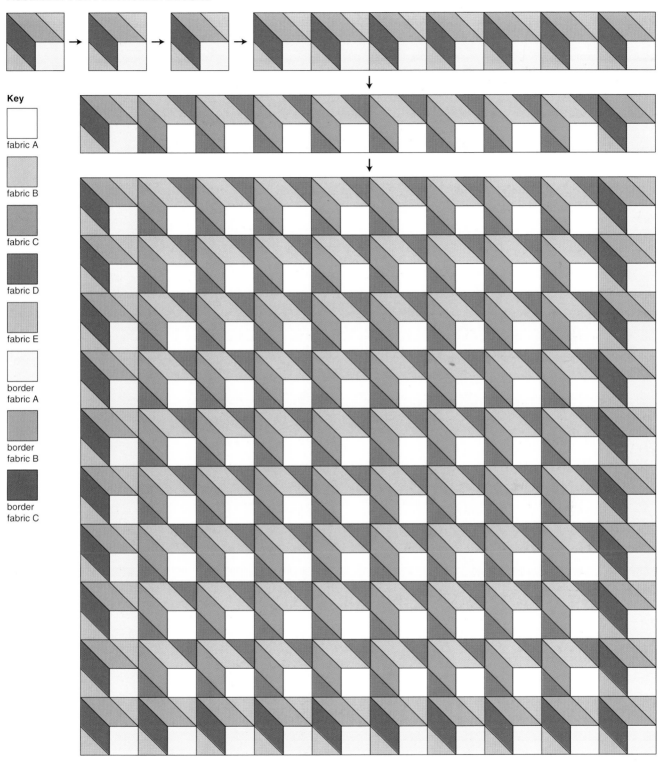

Key

fabric A

fabric B

fabric C

fabric D

fabric E

border
fabric A

border
fabric B

border
fabric C

Finishing the quilt

Press the assembled quilt top. Layer the quilt top, batting and backing, and baste (see page 147). For the Pink version, quilt in-the-ditch around the outside of each 'cube'. For the Blue version, stipple quilt in all template-X background triangles.

For both versions, trim the quilt edge and attach the binding (see page 148). Sew a button to the centre of each square patch.

Taupe Lattice Quilt

There are probably many for whom the palette of the Taupe Lattice is a favourite. The restraint in this colour scheme does help the eye zero in on the subtle beauty of shells and stones depicted in the prints.

It was surprising how colourful this patchwork looked on a monotone beach. The more I study these warm beige tones, the more depth they appear to have. The soft-coloured accents really sing out of the ground of quiet colours. I will always love the clashing of strong patterned fabrics for some effects, but this calmer taupe structure is slowly winning me over.

The deep ochre grounding of the Ochre Lattice creates such a mysterious old gold, Byzantine mood (see page 122) and is a much stronger statement than the Taupe version.

Size of quilt

The finished Taupe Lattice Quilt measures 68½in x 94in (174cm x 239cm). The Ochre Lattice version measures the same. *Note that the quilting will slightly reduce the final measurements.*

Taupe Lattice colour recipe

The lattice in this scheme is made entirely from a solid-coloured taupe fabric (fabric A). The large square patches inside the lattice are small- and medium-scale prints, mini-plaids and stripes, in beiges, taupes, camels, rose-beige and grey-lavender (fabric B). The small squares between the lattice pieces are solid-coloured fabrics and subtle monochromatic prints in peach, rose, mauve, sage, toffee and lavender (fabric C).

Alternative colour recipe

Ochre Lattice (page 122): In this alternative colour scheme the lattice is made entirely from an olive paisley print with deep gold and burgundy accents (fabric A).

The contrasting square patches inside the lattice are subtle small-scale monochromatic prints, plaids and stripes, in medium tones of periwinkle, burgundy, camel, deep green, pumpkin and steel blues (fabric B).

The small squares between the lattice pieces are solid-coloured fabrics and monochromatic prints in brilliant fuchsias, oranges, reds, blues and greens (fabric C).

Materials

44–45in (112cm) wide 100% cotton fabrics:
• *Fabric A* (lattice fabric): 3¼yd (3m) of a single fabric
• *Fabric B:* scraps of an assortment of fabrics in the colours in *Colour Recipe*
• *Fabric C:* scraps of an assortment of fabrics in the colours in *Colour Recipe*
• *Backing fabric:* 4¾yd (4.5m)
• *Outer-binding fabric:* ¾yd (70cm) of a striped fabric
Plus the following materials:
• Cotton batting, at least 3in (7.5cm) larger all around than finished pieced quilt top
• Cotton quilting thread

Patch shapes

The centre of the quilt is made from a single rectangular lattice patch (template S) and a large and small square patch (templates T and U). The border is made from a rectangular lattice patch (template V) and a large and small square patch (templates W and X).

RIGHT The Taupe Lattice Quilt in soft morning light on Winchelsea beach in England.

The actual-size templates for this quilt are given on page 153.

SPECIAL NOTE The border is designed to exactly fit the quilt centre, so do not try to alter the size of the quilt centre.

Cutting

Template S: cut 384 from fabric A.

Template T: cut 213 fabric B.

Template U: cut 212 from fabric C.

Template V: cut 132 from fabric A.

Template W: cut 44 from fabric B.

Template X: cut 92 from fabric C and 12 from fabric A.

SPECIAL NOTE Although the edges of the centre of the quilt have partial squares, full squares are used and the edges are trimmed off after the centre has been assembled.

Assembling the quilt centre

Following the assembly diagram on the opposite page, arrange the centre of the quilt, placing the lattice pieces and the small squares in between the large squares. Using the seam allowance marked on the templates throughout the quilt assembly, sew the patches together in diagonal rows, alternating rows of lattice and large squares with rows of lattice and small squares as shown. Join the diagonal rows together.

After the centre has been completed, trim the outside edge, making sure that you leave enough extra fabric along the edge for the seam allowance.

Making the borders

Following the diagram on page 108, join the template-V lattice pieces and the small template-X squares to make the four strips for border no. 1. Join the sides of border no. 1 to the quilt centre, then join the top and bottom strips.

TRIMMING QUILT CENTRE

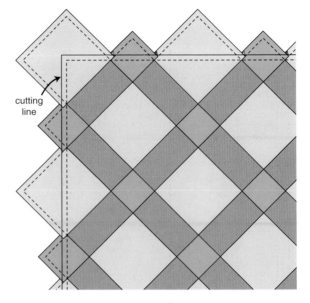

cutting line

Next, join the template-V lattice pieces, the template-W squares and the template-X squares to make the four strips for border no. 2. Join the top and bottom strips to the quilt, then join the side strips.

Lastly, join the template-V lattice pieces and the template-X squares to make the four strips for border no. 3. Join the sides to the quilt, then join the top and bottom.

Finishing the quilt

Press the quilt top. Layer the quilt top, batting and backing, and baste (see page 147). Quilt in-the-ditch of each seam line between the patches. Then stipple quilt the template-S and template-V lattice patches only (fabric A). Trim the quilt edge and attach the binding (see page 148).

QUILTING FOR TAUPE LATTICE

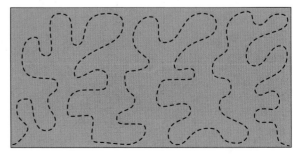

QUILT CENTRE ASSEMBLY

TEMPLATES FOR QUILT CENTRE

template S   template T   template U

TEMPLATES FOR QUILT BORDER

template V   template W   template X

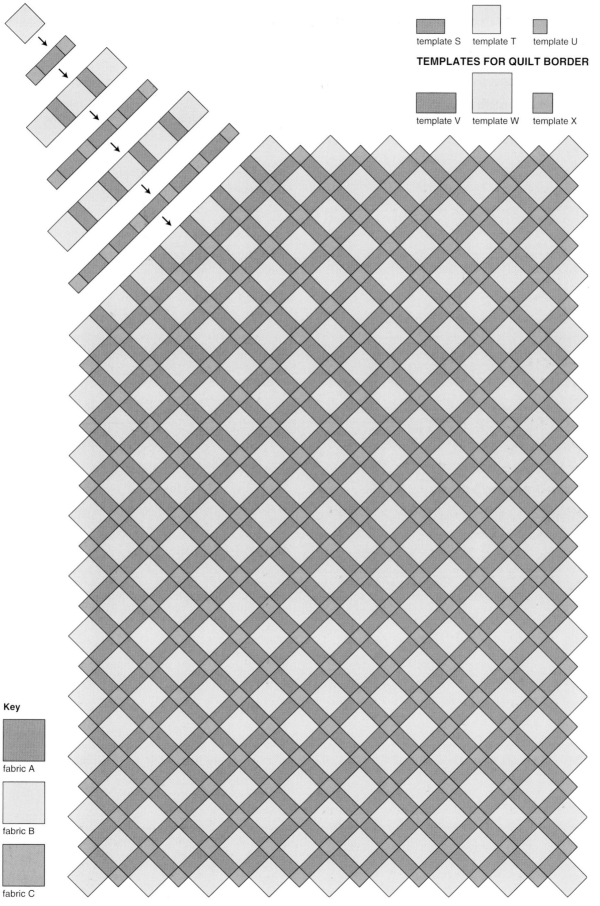

Key

fabric A

fabric B

fabric C

JOINING BORDERS

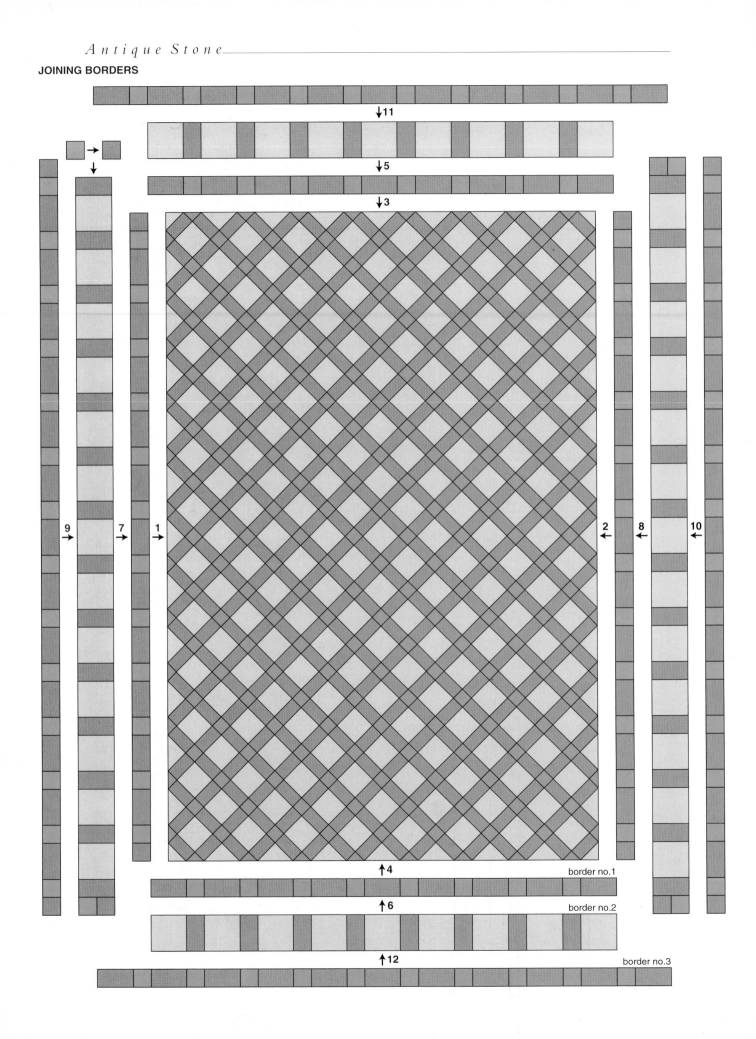

↓11

↓5

↓3

9 → 7 → 1 → 2 ← 8 ← 10 ←

↑4

border no.1

↑6

border no.2

↑12

border no.3

ABOVE The Taupe Lattice Quilt. See page 122 for the Ochre version.

Marble Venetian Tile Quilt

A big, bold square of squares, the Marble Venetian Tile Quilt was taken from a marble floor in St Marks Cathedral in Venice. In some ways it was the hardest patchwork to pick fabrics for. They needed to have a marble-like quality, come in contrasting light and dark versions, and have a variation in colour without loosing that old worn marble feel.

I felt the dynamic blocks would be hemmed in by a border, so let them go unrestricted to the edge of the quilt. Fonthill, with its multi-coloured tiles in earthy tones and romantic arched structure, hit just the right note as a setting for the quilt (see page 92).

The cathedral in Venice has a floor that is stuffed with ideas for textile designers. The colours and geometry of the cut stone can make you quite giddy as you walk around it. I picked one of the boldest geometric designs there and am amazed to see how changed it appears on the Striped version of the Venetian Tile patchwork (see page 121).

There are no instructions for the Striped Venetian Tile Quilt, but it uses the same templates as the Marble version. If you are keen, you could try making it by studying the photograph for the colour scheme. The centre square of each block is made in the same way as the Marble version, with a light, dark and two medium-toned triangles. But the outer border of trapezoids is added differently, with the two light-toned and two dark-toned parts of the frame adjacent.

Size of quilt

The finished Marble Venetian Tile Quilt measures 90½in x 99½in (230cm x 253cm). *Note that the quilting will slightly reduce the final measurements.*

Colour recipe

The overall colour scheme is that of marble tiles. The small triangles at the centre of each patchwork block are mono-chromatic prints in three tones of greys – an assortment of very similar greyish whites (fabric A), a single medium grey (fabric B) and an assortment of very similar charcoals (fabric C).

The trapezoid patches around the outside of each block are an assortment of solids, small-scale monochromatic prints, and mini-plaids and stripes that resemble the texture of stone and marble, in taupes, rose-beige, grey-lilac, ochres, steel blue, sage, sand and chalky sienna. Each of these trapezoid shades appears in a light tone (fabric D) and a corresponding medium tone (fabric E).

Materials

44–45in (112cm) wide 100% cotton fabrics:
• *Fabric A* (light tone in centre of each block): a total of ¾yd (70cm) of an assortment of fabrics
• *Fabric B* (medium tone in centre of each block): 1¼yd (1.2m) of a single fabric
• *Fabric C* (dark tone in centre of each block): a total of ¾yd (70cm) of an assortment of fabrics
• *Fabric D* (light tone on outside of each

RIGHT The Marble Venetian Tile Quilt in the magnificent tiled setting of Fonthill in Doylestown, Pennsylvania. (See page 92 for more about Henry Mercer's Fonthill 'castle'.)

block): scraps of an assortment of fabrics
• *Fabric E* (medium tone on outside
of each block): scraps of an assortment of
fabrics that match the colours of scraps of
fabric D, but are medium-toned
• *Backing fabric:* 6½ yd (6m)
• *Outer-binding fabric:* 1yd (1m) of a
mid-grey and black stripe
Plus the following materials:
• Cotton batting, at least 3in (7.5cm) larger
all around than finished pieced quilt top
(see page 147 for information on types of
batting to use)
• Cotton quilting thread

Patch shapes

The entire quilt is made using only two
patch shapes – a triangle (template S) that
forms the centre square of each block and
a trapezoid (template T) that forms the
outside of each block. The actual-size
templates are given on page 151.

Cutting

Fabric A (light tone in centre of each
block): cut 110 template-S triangles.
Fabric B (medium tone in centre of each
block): cut 220 template-S triangles.

BLOCK ASSEMBLY no.1

BLOCK ASSEMBLY no.2

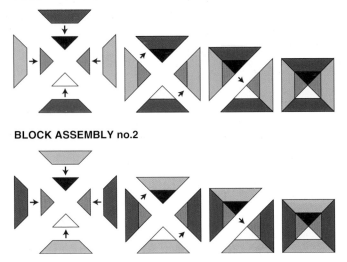

Fabric C (dark tone in centre of each
block): cut 110 template-S triangles.
Fabric D (light tone on outside of each
block): cut 110 matching pairs of template-
T trapezoids (making a total of 220
trapezoid patches).
Fabric E (medium tone on outside of
each block): cut 110 matching pairs of template-
T trapezoids (making a total of 220
patches) that match the colours of fabric-D
trapezoids, but are medium-toned.

Making the blocks

For the centre of the block, select four
template-S triangles – one in fabric A
(light-toned), one in fabric C (dark-toned)
and a matching pair in fabric B (medium-
toned). Then select four template-T
trapezoids – a matching pair in fabric D
(light-toned) and a matching pair in fabric
E (medium-toned) that are the same
colour as the fabric-D trapezoids.

Make a total of 110 blocks, arranging
half the blocks following the diagram
for block assembly no. 1 and half the
blocks following the diagram for block
assembly no. 2.
SPECIAL NOTE Join the patches of each
block in the order given in the block
assembly diagram and using the seam
allowance marked on the templates
throughout.

Assembling the blocks

Arrange the blocks in 11 rows of 10 blocks
each, keeping all the dark centre triangles
at the top and alternating the blocks with
the medium-toned outside trapezoids at
the top with the blocks with the light-
toned trapezoids at the top.

Join the blocks together in rows, then
join the rows together.

QUILT ASSEMBLY

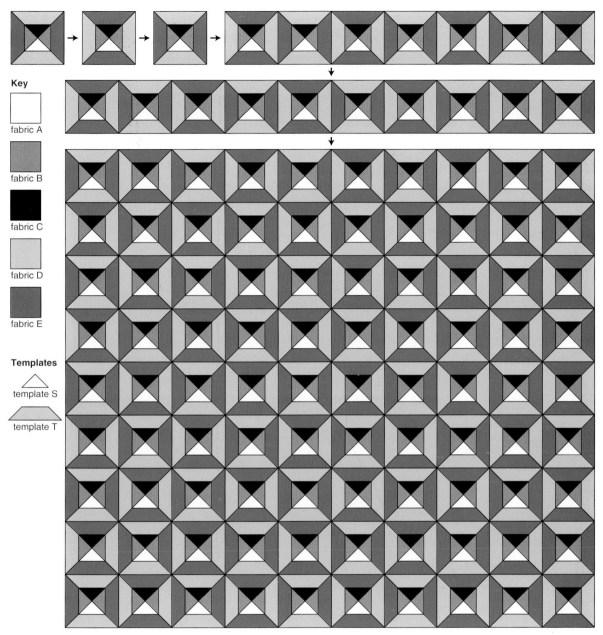

Key

fabric A

fabric B

fabric C

fabric D

fabric E

Templates

template S

template T

Finishing the quilt

Press the assembled quilt top. Layer the quilt top, batting and backing, and baste together (see page 147).

Quilt in-the-ditch along the two diagonal seam lines from corner to corner of each block. (See page 147 for how to choose quilting thread colours for your patchwork.)

Then stipple quilt the two light-toned trapezoid borders on every alternate block

and the medium-toned trapezoid borders on the remaining blocks (see pages 71 and 75 for examples of how to work random stipple quilting).

Trim the outer quilt edge to straighten the raw edge of the patchwork and to cut off any excess batting and backing. Then cut the binding strips on the bias from the striped binding fabric and attach (see page 148 for detailed instructions on making a double-fold binding).

Beige 4-patch curtains

When combined, large squares of velvets and brocades in washy grey-greens, peaches and pale ochres make quite a sumptuous set of drapes. We just glued the fabric in a crazy-patch manner on the wooden pelmet above the window, but the valance could be made in proper patchwork. You will notice that there are no really pale or dark fabrics; an overall medium softness is important for this stoney look.

The curtains were photographed in the Kaffe Fassett Designs shop in Bath (see right). The two panels on either side of the patchwork curtains are antique American hooked rugs. My shell needlepoint chair looks very comfortable in this delicate, elusive palette.

Because of the substantial weight of the brocades and velvets, this patchwork would make a wonderful couch cover or bedspread. And large cushions in the 4-patch layout would complement either of these perfectly.

Size of curtains

Each of the two finished patchwork curtain panels measures 48in x 60in (120cm x 150cm). *Note that the metric size will not exactly match the imperial size.*

Colour recipe

This colour scheme includes light tones of terracotta-pink, cool sages, sand, taupe and camels. The materials used are medium-weight furnishing/upholstery fabrics in velvets, damasks, floral prints and chenilles.

The directions give detailed instructions for working with furnishing/upholstery fabrics.

Materials

- *Patch fabric:* Assorted pieces of furnishing/upholstery fabrics in the colours outlined in the *Colour Recipe*
- *Lining:* 2yd (1.7m) of 54in (137cm) wide fabric for each panel
- Clip-on rings for hanging curtain

SPECIAL NOTE Do not wash furnishing/upholstery fabrics before use as you would cotton fabrics.

Patch shapes

The entire patchwork is made from only 3 sizes of square patches – large, medium and small. The finished patches measure 12in (30cm), 6in (15cm) and 4in (10cm) square.

Cutting

Large squares: cut 18 large squares each measuring $12\frac{1}{2}$in x $12\frac{1}{2}$in (31.5cm x 31.5cm) for each curtain panel.

Medium-sized squares: cut 16 pairs of matching medium-sized squares each measuring $6\frac{1}{2}$in x $6\frac{1}{2}$in (16.5cm x 16.5cm) for each curtain panel (a total of 32 squares).

Small squares: cut a total of 91 small squares each measuring $4\frac{1}{2}$in x $4\frac{1}{2}$in (11.5cm x 11.5cm) for each curtain panel, cutting 9 sets of four matching squares, and 9 sets of five matching squares.

SPECIAL NOTE The cutting sizes given above include the seam allowance which is $\frac{1}{4}$in (7.5mm).

RIGHT The Beige 4-patch Curtains and the Waterlily needlepoint cushion in the Kaffe Fassett Designs shop in Bath. (See page 159 for information on Ehrman needlepoint kits.)

4-PATCH BLOCK ASSEMBLY

9-PATCH BLOCK ASSEMBLY

CURTAIN ASSEMBLY

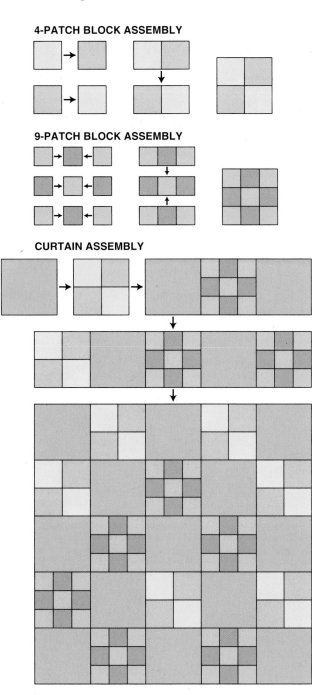

Preparing the cut patches

Since furnishing/upholstery fabrics usually fray quite easily, the raw edges should be finished before the patches are joined. Finish the edges by zigzag stitching on a sewing machine or by overlocking.

Making the 4-patch blocks

Select two medium-sized squares of the same fabric and two medium-sized squares

the same of another fabric. Using a $\frac{1}{4}$ in (7.5mm) seam allowance throughout the making of the patchwork, make a 4-patch block, joining as shown in the diagram. Make a total of eight 4-patch blocks for each curtain panel.

SPECIAL NOTE Because furnishing/ upholstery fabrics are bulkier than ordinary cotton patchwork fabrics, all seams should be pressed open during the making of the patchwork to eliminate bulk at the seam intersections.

Making the 9-patch blocks

Select four small squares of the same fabric and 5 small squares the same of another fabric. Make a 9-patch block, joining as shown in the diagram. Make a total of nine 9-patch blocks for each curtain panel.

Assembling the blocks

Arrange the eight 4-patch blocks, the nine 9-patch blocks and the 10 large squares into five separate rows as shown in the diagram. Join the blocks together in rows, then join the rows together.

Finishing the curtains

Press the assembled patchwork and trim around the outside edge to straighten it.

Make the lining to the same size as the curtain panel, if necessary, piecing as you would a patchwork backing (see page 147 for piecing advice).

Lay the lining face down and smooth out. Then lay the curtain panel on top of the lining with the wrong sides facing. Turn the seam allowances to the inside around the edge of the curtain and the lining, pinning and basting the turned under edges together. Topstitch the pieces together and remove the basting threads.

ABOVE The Beige 4-patch Curtains are made from large square patches of upholstery/furnishing-weight velvets, damasks, floral prints and chenilles.

Renaissance

Renaissance is for me burgundy velvets, bold brocades, stained glass brilliance and huge heraldic strength of design. This chapter is for romantic souls who love drama and strong statements. These are patchwork quilts that would suit deep-toned rooms with great pots of dark flowers, collections of strongly coloured ceramics and tiles, and mosaic details. The Renaissance style I have in mind is certainly not about minimal restrained taste, it's about extravagant overkill and courageous use of colour – as in a room I saw in Edinburgh that had deep lemon walls, a luxuriant mahogany table and a large pot of brilliant burgundy pansies. Or an extraordinary room in a London town house created by Anoushka Hempel that had forest green marble floors, black walls, and huge flat bowls of dark purple anenomies glowing under dramatic spotlights.

FACING PAGE The sumptuous detail from an early eighteenth-century painting by Jean Francois de Troy (top left) is the mood I was after for my Brocade and Velvet Throw (top right). The Jewel Floating Blocks Quilt (bottom left) and Ochre Lattice Quilt (bottom right) were both shot at botanical illustrator Anne Marie Evans' country house.

ABOVE The Striped Diamonds Quilt at Fonthill. RIGHT The Jewel Floating Blocks (see page 95 for instructions). FACING PAGE The flaming autumn Virginia creeper at the American Museum in Bath reflects gloriously on to the Striped Venetian Tile Table Cover.

When people tell me they are afraid of colour or don't feel qualified to arrange it, I imagine they mean bright colours like the ones used in this chapter, which deals with what I call 'committed colour'. Strong, saturated colour can make the heart sing and the pulse quicken, but equally it can upset and jar if the tones aren't in harmony. To me, arranging colour is not an intellectual process, it is a matter of mixing shades instinctively and removing the ones that seem to steal the show or over-shadow the others. Often a light colour will contrast too harshly with a strong, deep palette. When removed, the deeper colour will begin to dance and vibrate in a richer manner.

The fewer rules one has, the better, since sometimes an unpredictable combination will spark a colour group. When we photographed the quilts for this book we carried many patchworks around to locations and often the best results occurred when spotting some unexpected colour in a garden or on a painted wall and just trying the quilt against it to see if it lived or died. You can judge for yourself which shots succeeded.

The Striped Diamonds Quilt (above left) makes use of fabrics I designed to be woven in India (see page 92). I like the way the stripes square off, making various-sized boxes from a simple diamond layout (see diagram on page 80).

Jewel Floating Blocks (above) demonstrates once again how powerful stained-glass colours are intensified when surrounded by shades of blacks. We see it here in the garden of the botanical illustrator Anne Marie Evans. The needlepoint of roses in the shot was a giant effort between us both.

The Striped Venetian Tile Table Cover (right) surprises me each time I remember that it is the same layout as the Marble

ABOVE The Ochre Lattice Quilt (see page 104 for instructions) with my Ribbon
Nosegay needlepoint cushion. RIGHT The Burgundy Tents Wall Hanging.

Venetian Tile version (see page 111). Here I
have used my Indian weaves, but positioned
them horizontally to create exciting striped
frames around the blocks. The deep saturated
blue, maroon and pinkness of this colour
scheme are delightful.

The Ochre Lattice Quilt (above) was the
first quilt that Liza and I made that really
created the glow I was after. The constant
shades of old golden ochre as a base make
the little jewel 'studs' at the corners gleam
like stones in a Byzantine crown. Often
when doing arrangements of shades of one
colour, there is a definite need for a kick
colour or two. Otherwise, dozens of reds
and pinks can look like two colours. In
order for a background to settle and let the
foreground shapes read, there should be

some unity to it. Picking all reds and dark
wine tones for the Burgundy Tents (right)
helps the various stripes in the tents make
an impression. Having said that, you can see
that I always favour a little merging of fore-
and background to add mysterious corners
and softness. I learned this from studying
old faded fabrics and peeling walls where
partially obscured patterns have great charm.

Burgundy Tents is a far easier patchwork
to make than the Circus Tents version on
page 57. You just cut striped fabric patches
for the square bottom of the tent and the
triangular top, instead of piecing the stripes.
I have used the deeper colours of my Indian
woven stripes collection for the tents and
surrounded them with a 'sky' of dark burgundies, rusts and maroons.

Brocade and Velvet Throw

The secret of this luxurious textile throw is to get enough variety in your velvets and brocades. I kept the tones quite similar in value while gathering a wide range of plums, earthy browns, ochres and forest greens in furnishing- or upholstery-weight fabric.

I found my fabrics in the glorious ABC Carpet and Home store on Broadway at 19th Street in New York. It is one of the most inspiring stores – six floors of romantic furniture, bedding, carpets, fabrics, crockery, mosaic tables, shell-covered items, etc. There are so many unusual colour and texture ideas around every corner that you can't help being stimulated.

Because of the weight of these furnishing fabrics I wouldn't attempt to use them for intricate patches, like those of tumbling blocks for instance. But for these simple large squares they are perfect.

The romantic setting for the throw is a friend's room, which brings together deliciously unexpected but ideal objects to accompany this throw. What a stunning variety of roses, painted, printed, embroidered, dried and real! Though this room is crowded with visual textures and pattern it creates a very mellow ambiance. The richness of the brocade and velvet throw is right at home here.

Size of throw

The finished patchwork throw measures 60in x 60in (150cm x 150cm). *Note that the metric size of the throw will not exactly match the imperial size.*

Colour recipe

This colour scheme includes deep tones of plums, camel, golds, moss and forest greens, and burgundies. The materials used are furnishing/upholstery-weight fabrics in velvets, damasks, fruit prints, paisley weaves and chenilles.

Materials

- *Patch fabric:* Assorted pieces of furnishing/upholstery fabrics
- *Backing fabric:* $2^3/4$ yd (2.5m) of 44in (122cm) wide fabric
- 7yd (6.5m) of $^1/2$ in (12mm) wide dark green grosgrain ribbon

SPECIAL NOTE Do not wash furnishing/upholstery fabrics before use.

Patch shapes

The entire patchwork is made from only two sizes of square patches – large and small. The finished patches measure 12in (30cm) and 6in (15cm) square.

Cutting

Large squares: cut 13 large squares each measuring $12^1/2$ in x $12^1/2$ in (31.5cm x 31.5cm).

Small squares: cut 24 pairs of matching small squares each measuring $4^1/2$ in x $4^1/2$ in (11.5cm x 11.5cm) for a total of 48 squares.

SPECIAL NOTE The cutting sizes include the seam allowance.

Preparing the cut patches

Since furnishing/upholstery fabrics usually fray quite easily, the raw edges should be

RIGHT The multitude of roses – painted, porcelain, beaded, dried and real – make a luscious, romantic setting for the Brocade and Velvet Throw.

ABOVE The Brocade and Velvet Throw was made with furnishing/upholstery fabrics.

4-PATCH BLOCK ASSEMBLY

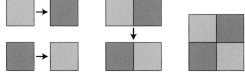

THROW ASSEMBLY

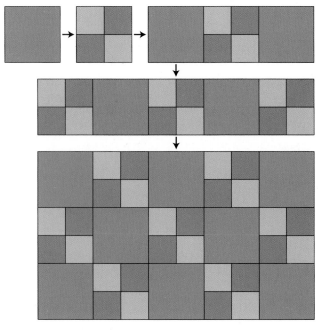

finished before the patches are joined. Finish the edges around each patch by zigzag stitching on the sewing machine or by overlocking.

Making the 4-patch blocks

Select two medium-sized squares of the same fabric and two medium-sized squares the same of another fabric. Using a $\frac{1}{4}$ in (7.5mm) seam allowance throughout the making of the patchwork, make a 4-patch block, joining as shown in the diagram.

Make a total of 12 4-patch blocks, occasionally making a 'mistake' in the block by mismatching the pairs of squares to add variety to the layout.

SPECIAL NOTE Because furnishing/upholstery fabrics are bulkier than ordinary cotton patchwork fabrics, all seams should be pressed open during the making of the patchwork to eliminate bulk at the seam intersections.

Assembling the blocks

Arrange the 12 4-patch blocks and the 13 large squares into five separate rows as shown in the diagram. Join the patches together in rows, then join the rows.

Finishing the throw

Press the assembled patchwork. Make the backing to the same size as the patchwork (see page 147). Then lay the backing on top of the patchwork with the wrong sides facing and pin. With the backing facing, baste the grosgrain ribbon around the edge so that $\frac{1}{4}$ in (6mm) of the ribbon extends past the raw edges. Machine stitch the ribbon in place close to the edge. Turn the ribbon to the right side of the throw, then baste and topstitch in place. Remove the basting threads.

Gridlock Quilt

I first spotted this 'gridlock' layout of squares in a book on old carpets. It was a dream to knit and I used it first for a waistcoat, then went on to knit a jacket and crewneck for my *California Patches* collection.

Liza loved the geometry too and adapted my knitting into patchwork using the colours from my original waistcoat. She brought it off in great style, and I feel it is one of the strongest quilts in this collection. The striped colour changes in the big squares relate to the knitted yarn changes in my waistcoat. Couldn't you imagine a quite soft version of this in old stone shades? You could make a very chalky, subtle quilt for an elegant off-white interior.

Size of quilt

The finished patchwork quilt measures $68^{1}/_{2}$ in x $80^{1}/_{2}$ in (171.5cm x 201.5cm). *Note that the metric size will not exactly match the imperial size and that the quilting will slightly reduce the final measurements.*

Colour recipe

The checkerboard blocks are made of a dark group of colours and a light group. Most of the darks are navy, brown-black, and deep teal; and the remainder are magenta, purple, royal blue and rust. The lights are pumpkin, rose-beige, lavender, lilac, periwinkle, plum, sage and aqua. The colours are arranged so that each horizontal line in the checkerboard has the same two colours, and often these two tones are used for one, two, three or four rows.

The 'strip' blocks with the square in the centre should look as though they have been made of one outside colour that has been faded and streaked. The small inside square is a solid-coloured fabric, and the background is made of strips of related colours so that it appears that the small square is floating on top of the big square. The colours used for the 'strip' blocks (and the squares border) are the same colours as those used for the checkerboard blocks.

The fabrics are a selection of solids, tie dyes, small-scale monochromatic prints, subtle stripes and mini-plaids.

Materials

44–45in (112cm) wide 100% cotton fabrics:
• *Patch fabric:* Scraps in the assortment of colours outlined in the *Colour Recipe*
• *Backing fabric*: 4yd (4m)
• *Outer-binding fabric:* $^{3}/_{4}$ yd (70cm) of a dark stripe
Plus the following materials:
• Cotton batting, at least 3in (7.5cm) larger all around than finished pieced quilt top
• Cotton quilting thread

Patch shapes

Most of the quilt is made from two sizes of square patches. The finished patches measure 4in (10cm) square and 2in (5cm) square. The larger square is used for the border and for the centre of the 'strip' blocks. The smaller square is used for the checkerboard blocks.

The only other patch shape used is the narrow strips of random width that make up the background of the 'strip' blocks.

Cutting

Small checkerboard squares: cut 270 squares each measuring $2^{1}/_{2}$ in x $2^{1}/_{2}$ in (6.5cm x

OVERLEAF The rich colours of old boats on the Hastings beach in England create a superb backdrop for the Gridlock Quilt.

6.5cm) from the light fabrics and 270 from the dark fabrics.

'Strip' blocks: cut 15 squares each measuring $4\frac{1}{2}$ in x $4\frac{1}{2}$ in (11.5cm x 11.5cm) from the light fabrics and dark fabrics at random; cut the background strips in random widths as the blocks are pieced.

Border: cut 70 squares each measuring $4\frac{1}{2}$ in x $4\frac{1}{2}$ in (11.5cm x 11.5cm), cutting about half from the light fabrics and half from the dark fabrics (to allow for 'mistake' squares). SPECIAL NOTE All cutting sizes include the seam allowance.

Making the checkerboard blocks

Alternating the light and dark colours, arrange 18 small dark squares and 18 small light squares in 6 rows of 6 squares as shown in the diagram. Use the same two colours in each horizontal row and use the same two colours for one to four rows.

When assembling the patches, use a $\frac{1}{4}$ in (7.5mm) seam allowance throughout. Join the patches together in rows, then join the rows together. Make a total of 15 blocks.

Making the 'strip' blocks

Using the light and dark colours at random for these blocks, select a single large $4\frac{1}{2}$ in (11.5cm) square for the centre. Choose a contrasting colour for the background around the square, then pick related tones to accent this colour. Cutting strips of random widths, sew these related colours together to make two pieces each measuring $4\frac{1}{2}$ in x $12\frac{1}{2}$ in (11.5cm x 31.5cm) for the top and bottom of the block. Then make one piece measuring $4\frac{1}{2}$ in x 9in (11.5cm x 23cm) and cut it in half to form the two sides of the block each measuring $4\frac{1}{2}$ in x $4\frac{1}{2}$ in (11.5cm x 11.5cm). Sew the two sides of the block to the centre

square, then join the top and bottom. Make a total of 15 'strip' blocks, occasionally using a single piece of fabric for the side, top or bottom of the block.

Assembling the blocks

Following the diagram, arrange the 15 checkerboard blocks and the 15 'strip' blocks into six separate rows with the blocks alternating. Join the blocks together in rows, then join the rows together.

Making the border

Alternating the light and dark colours (but with a few 'mistakes'), make two border strips of 15 of the $4\frac{1}{2}$ in (11.5cm) squares, and two border strips of 20 squares. Sew the shorter strips to the top and bottom of the quilt, then stitch the longer strips to the sides of the quilt.

Finishing the quilt

Press the quilt top. Layer the quilt top, batting and backing, and baste (see page 147).

Using many differently coloured threads that match the top, stipple quilt the large background square of each 'strip' block and the border squares, and quilt concentric squares in the centre square of the 'strip' block. Quilt the checkerboard blocks in-the-ditch. Attach the binding (see page 148).

QUILTING

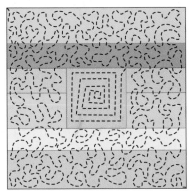

'STRIP'-BLOCK ASSEMBLY

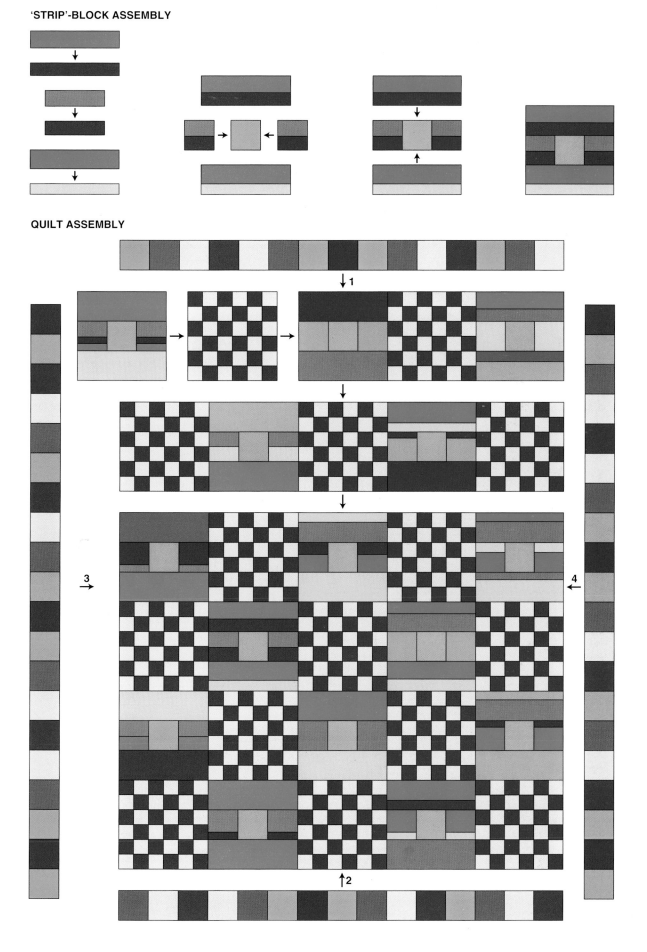

QUILT ASSEMBLY

Scarlet and Emerald 2-by-2 Table Cover

There are times in life when one craves the deepest, most saturated colours. When I first saw this brilliant display of scarlet and high green in the completed patchwork, I thought of my friend Anne Marie Evans' green dining room in her country house. The old oak furniture, oriental carpet and deep crimson flowers set the quilt off to perfection (right). The stripe borders work a treat on this patchwork, and the stipple quilting reserved for the green areas makes the reds and pinks pop.

When I finished this design I heard there was quite a tradition for green and red patchworks in America. Most of the ones I have seen have large areas of white in them which creates a very different effect.

The 2-by-2 is a patchwork formula I return to again and again. It was a design I kept coming across in collections of old quilts, and it astounded me how fresh it always looked as it changed with every new colour scheme. (See page 17 for the Pastel 2-by-2 version and pages 2 and 37 for the Citrus and Delft 2-by-2 version.)

Size of table cover
The finished Red and Green 2-by-2 table cover (or quilt) measures 72$\frac{1}{2}$in x 89$\frac{1}{2}$in (184cm x 227cm). The Pastel 2-by-2 version measures the same. The Citrus and Delft version is a table cover and measures 72$\frac{1}{2}$in (184cm) square. *Note that the quilting will slightly reduce the final measurements.*

Scarlet and Emerald colour recipe
Each 4-patch block in the quilt centre is made up of two fabrics – two patches from each of the two fabric groups. The first group (fabric A) is mostly reds of all kinds, from tomato to raspberry and magenta, with a sprinkling of a few 'mistake' oranges. The second group (fabric B) is mostly greens of all kinds, from bottle to sage and teal, with a sprinkling of turquoise and airforce blue. Both groups are solids, small-scale multi-coloured and monochromatic prints, and mini-plaids and stripes.

The fabric for the border triangles is a bold navy and bright green stripe. The outer border strips are a multi-coloured stripe predominantly in dusty reds, pinks, sage and lavender, and the border corner squares are leftover scraps from the centre.

Alternate colour recipes
Pastel 2-by-2 (page 17): Fabric A is mostly light neutral beiges and creams, and a sprinkling of a few 'maverick' pale pinks and taupes. *Fabric B* is mostly chalky pastels in pale peachy pink, robin's egg blue, butter, sage, lilac, grey-blue, lavenders and browns, with a sprinkling of a few 'mistake' tones. Both colour groups are a mixture of solids, small-scale multi-coloured and monochromatic prints, and mini-plaids and stripes.

The fabric for the border triangles has a pale pinky beige ground with mid brown stripes. The fabric for the outer border strips is ecru with rose polka dots.
Citrus and Delft 2-by-2 (page 37): Half the *fabric-A group* is acid yellows, dull golds,

RIGHT The Scarlet and Emerald 2-by-2 Table Cover glowing in Anne Marie Evans' handsome green dining room.

ABOVE The Scarlet and Emerald 2-by-2. See page 2 and page 17 for the other colourways.

peach and lime and the other half is blue-and-whites and light blues.

The acid yellows, dull golds, peach and lime are solid-coloured fabrics and French Provincal prints. The blue-and-whites are plaids, small-scale prints and 'toile' prints. The light blues are stripes, checks and small-scale monochromatic prints.

Half of the *fabric-B group* is a single Delft-blue fabric and the other half is a range of deep blues. The deep blues are plaids, Provincal prints and monochromatic prints. The Delft-blue fabric is a large paisley printed on a white background.

When making the blocks, pair the acid yellows, dull golds, peach and lime with the Delft paisley, and the blue-and-whites and light blues with the deep blues.

TEMPLATES

template W   template X   template Y

BLOCK ASSEMBLY

The fabric for the border triangles is the same Delft paisley that is used in the fabric-B colour group.

The fabric for the outer border strips and the border corners squares is a bold blue-on-blue floral print.

Materials

44–45in (112cm) wide 100% cotton fabrics:

Scarlet and Emerald version
• *Fabrics A and B:* scraps of an assortment of fabrics in the colours outlined in the *Colour Recipe* on page 132
• *Border-triangle fabric:* 1¼ yd (1.2m)
• *Outer-border fabric:* ¾ yd (70m) of a striped fabric
• *Backing:* 4yd (4m)
• *Outer-binding fabric:* 1yd (1m) of a stripe

Pastel version
• *Fabrics A and B:* scraps of an assortment of fabrics in the colours outlined in the *Colour Recipe* on page 132
• *Border-triangle fabric:* 1¼ yd (1.2m) of a striped fabric
• *Outer-border fabric:* ¾ yd (70m) of a polka dot fabric
• *Backing:* 4yd (4m)
• *Outer-binding:* 1yd (1m) of a stripe

Citrus and Delft version
• *Fabrics A and B:* scraps of an assortment of fabrics in the colours and prints outlined in the *Colour Recipe* which is

ASSEMBLY FOR SCARLET AND EMERALD VERSION

given on pages 132 and 134
• *Border-triangle fabric:* 1¼yd (1.2m) of blue paisley used in fabric-B colour group
• *Outer-border fabric:* ¾yd (70m) of a bold blue-on-blue floral print
Scarlet and Emerald version and Pastel version
• Cotton batting, at least 3in (7.5cm) larger

all around than finished pieced quilt top
• Green cotton quilting thread for Scarlet and Emerald version, beige for Pastel version

Patch shapes

The patchwork is made from only three patch shapes – a square that is used for the entire quilt centre (template W), and two sizes of triangle for the triangle border (template X and Y). The finished square patch measures 3in x 3in (7.5cm x 7.5cm). See page 155 for the actual-size templates.

Cutting

Follow the cutting instructions for your chosen version of the 2-by-2 quilt.

Scarlet and Emerald version

Template W: cut 286 squares from fabric A and 286 squares from fabric B.

SPECIAL NOTE Cut the following border triangles (templates X and Y) and border strips so that the stripes will radiate out from the centre of the patchwork.

Template X: from the border-triangle fabric, cut 32 large triangles.

Template Y: from the border-triangle fabric, cut 4 small triangles.

Border strips: from the outer-border fabric, cut two strips $2\frac{1}{2}$in x $68\frac{1}{2}$in (6.5cm x 174cm) for the top and bottom borders and two strips $2\frac{1}{2}$in x $85\frac{1}{2}$in (6.5cm x 217cm) for the two side borders.

Border corners: from fabric A or B, cut 4 squares $2\frac{1}{2}$in x $2\frac{1}{2}$in (6.5cm x 6.5cm).

Pastel version

Template W: cut 286 squares from fabric A and 286 squares from fabric B.

SPECIAL NOTE Cut the border triangles (templates X and Y) so that the stripes run parallel to the sides of the patchwork.

Template X: from the border-triangle fabric, cut 32 large triangles.

Template Y: from the border-triangle fabric, cut 4 small triangles.

Border strips: from the outer-border fabric, cut two strips $2\frac{1}{2}$in x $72\frac{1}{2}$in (6.5cm x 184cm) for the top and bottom borders and two strips $2\frac{1}{2}$in x $85\frac{1}{2}$in (6.5cm x 217cm) for the two side borders.

Citrus and Delft version

Template W: cut 160 squares from the fabric-A 'yellows' group and 126 squares from fabric-A light blues or whites; cut 160 squares from fabric-B Delft blue and 126 squares from fabric-B deep blues.

Template X: from the border-triangle fabric, cut 28 large triangles.

Template Y: from the border-triangle fabric, cut 4 small triangles.

Border strips: from the outer-border fabric, cut two strips $2\frac{1}{2}$in x $68\frac{1}{2}$in (6.5cm x 174cm) for the side borders and two strips $2\frac{1}{2}$in x $72\frac{1}{2}$in (6.5cm x 184cm) for the top and bottom borders.

Making the blocks

Select two template-W squares of the same fabric A and two squares of the same fabric B. Using the seam allowance marked on the templates throughout and joining as shown in the diagram given on page 134, make a four-patch block. Make a total of 143 four-patch blocks for the Scarlet and Emerald version and the Pastel version, and 113 for the Citrus and Delft version.

Assembling the blocks

Following the diagram, arrange the blocks so that the fabric-A patches point up and down and the fabric-B patches point side to side. Arrange the border triangles around the blocks. Join the patches together in diagonal rows, then join the diagonal rows together.

Making the border

For the Scarlet and Emerald version only, join the border corner squares to the top and bottom borders. For all versions, join the side border strips to the centre panel, then sew on the top and bottom borders.

ASSEMBLY FOR CITRUS AND DELFT VERSION

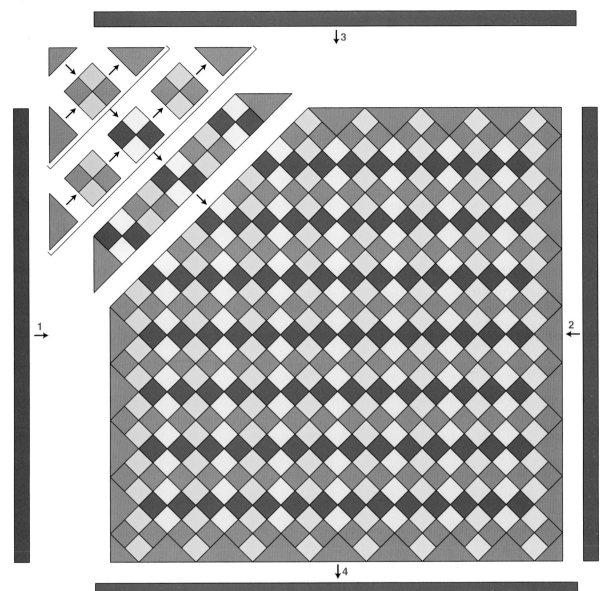

QUILTING

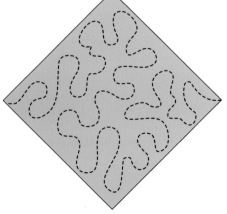

Finishing the quilt

Press the patchwork. For the Citrus and Delft version, turn under the edge and stitch. For the other versions, layer the quilt top, batting and backing, and baste. On the Scarlet and Emerald version, stipple quilt in the 'green' square patches only; and on the Pastel version, in the 'beige' square patches only. For both, quilt in-the-ditch around the border triangles and between the triangles and the outer border. Trim the quilt edge and attach the binding (see page 148).

Jewel Squares Blind

In my book *Glorious Interiors* I featured a great knitted throw that was many shades of red with kick colours of acid green and peacock blue. Liza had a go at translating it into patchwork and this magic square of squares resulted. I whisked it past a window just before she was about to quilt it and was so dazzled by the stained-glass effect that I forbade her to back it with anything other than a black gauze. We use it as a glowing jewelled curtain.

I have seen lampshades and other window shades made of unlined patchwork and feel it works a treat. The seams create a leading effect for your patchwork stained glass. This looks very daunting to construct, but using the paper foundation piecing method it is quite straight forward (I am told). The intricacy of it would make a stunningly detailed patchwork cushion cover or waistcoat.

This colour scheme is based on a rich assortment of reds but you could do it in blues, greens, or pinks or yellows for an equally enchanting rendition.

Size of window blind

The finished patchwork blind measures $42\frac{1}{2}$ in x $39\frac{1}{2}$ in (108cm x 100cm).

Colour recipe

At first glance the colours in this particular patchwork scheme appear to be very bright. In fact, although there are many bright colours and some neon colours, there are dull colours in the layout as well. The bright colours are various medium to dark reds, emerald greens, blues, magentas, oranges and purples.

The neons are chartreuse, yellow, orange and pink.

The dulls are plum, pumpkin, moss, rust, burgundy and chestnut. The fabrics are mini-plaids and small-scale monochromatic prints and paisleys.

Materials

• *Patch fabrics:* scraps in an assortment of cotton fabrics in the solid colours outlined in the *Colour Recipe* with half of the fabrics in the red family
• *Backing fabric:* 45in x 36in (114cm x 91cm) piece of black silk scrim
• 6yd (5.5m) of $\frac{1}{2}$in (12mm) wide dark red grosgrain ribbon
• Monofilament thread (clear nylon thread)

Patch shapes

The patchwork is made from six sizes of square blocks that are made up of fabric strips. The strips are sewn together to make the squares using the simple foundation-piecing method.

Foundation papers

The six foundation-paper squares (A, B, C, D, E and F) used for this quilt are given on pages 156–158. The instructions for foundation piecing are given on pages 146 and 147. Before beginning the quilt, make the required number of copies of each foundation square, using the various versions of the squares at random.
Block-A foundation paper: 68 copies.
Block-B foundation paper: 58 copies.
Block-C foundation paper: 18 copies.

RIGHT The Jewel Squares Window Blind beneath a collection of glass bottles.

<small>ABOVE</small> The Jewel Squares patchwork is made using the simple paper-foundation-piecing technique.

Block-D foundation paper: 9 copies.
Block-E foundation paper: 2 copies.
Block-F foundation paper: 2 copies.

Cutting strips for square blocks

Cut the fabric into strips of any length and in various widths from ¾in (2cm) to 2in (5cm). Cut only a few strips to begin with, then cut the remainder of the strips as they are needed.

Making the blocks

Using the foundation papers, make 68 A-blocks, 58 B-blocks, 18 C-blocks, nine D-blocks, two E-blocks and two F-blocks, following the instructions for foundation piecing on pages 146 and 147. Arrange the strips on the blocks so that concentric squares appear, by using the same fabric in each of the four sides of each concentric square. Occasionally use 'mistake' strips.

ASSEMBLY

Key

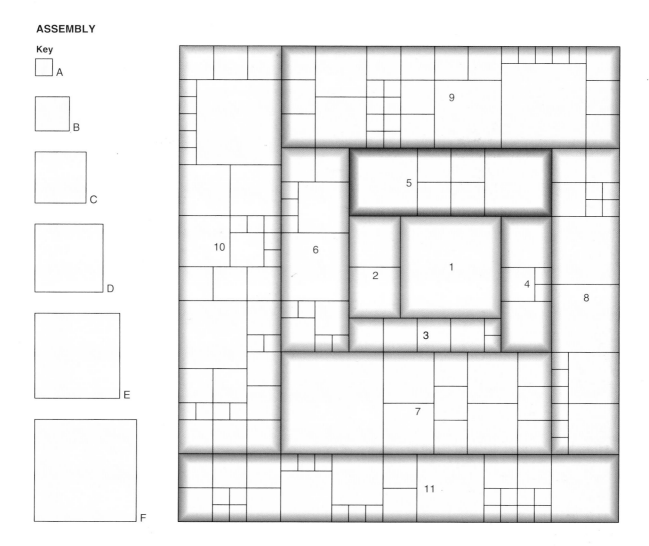

A

B

C

D

E

F

Most of these 'mistakes' should be subtle, and a few should be very obvious.

When choosing colours to place in each square, use the neons mostly for the very narrow strips. Be sure to put dull colours next to brights.

Assembling

When assembling the patchwork, use the seam allowance marked on the foundation papers throughout.

Following the diagram, arrange the blocks. Sew the blocks together in groups as shown. Starting with one F-block in the centre, sew group 2 to the centre, then group 3, and so on in the order given until all 11 groups are joined.

Finishing the window blind

Press the patchwork. Make the backing to the same size as the blind (see page 147). Lay the backing on top of the patchwork with the wrong sides facing and pin. With the patchwork facing and aligning one edge of the ribbon with the raw edge, baste the grosgrain ribbon around the edge stitching through the ribbon, patchwork and backing. Machine stitch $\frac{1}{4}$ in (6mm) from the edge. Remove the basting thread. Turn the ribbon to the wrong side of the blind and baste. Using nylon monofilament thread, topstitch in place stitching $\frac{1}{4}$ in (6mm) from the edge. Remove the basting threads. Sew small loops of grosgrain ribbon to the top edge for hanging.

Patchwork Basics

Patchwork techniques in their simplest forms can be very easy, and there are several designs in this book made entirely from squares. If you are a newcomer to patchwork, you could start with a 'squares' quilt such as Rosy (see page 69) or the Brocade and Velvet Throw (see page 125) and come up with delightful results. Or, if the prospect of such a large piece seems daunting, make your first patchwork project a cushion cover such as the Yellow Stripes (see page 46). With practice the techniques will become second nature, and you will be able to enjoy concentrating on playing with colours within a patchwork geometry.

The methods that follow are not meant to cover all the possible technical approaches to patchwork; they are merely the basics along with some very useful tips. Both hand piecing and machine piecing are covered. Those of you who want to carry your work with you may opt for the traditional hand piecing, but if you are keen on speedy results and have a sewing machine, you should try machine stitching your patchwork (see page 145).

I am not one for elaborate quilting stitches and prefer quilting that does not distract from the patchwork geometry and the play of colour and fabric pattern. Many of my quilts have the invisible stitch-in-the ditch quilting where the quilting stitches are worked into the seam lines and do not add another dimension to the quilt. Several projects, such as table covers, curtain panels, a window blind, a throw and a cushion cover have been left as simple patchwork with no quilting at all. (See page 147 for basic quilting directions).

My advice is always the following – try not to get bogged down by the techniques. Keep the experience of making patchworks a joyful one.

Patchwork Fabrics

One hundred per cent lightweight cotton fabrics, specially produced for quilts, are the best materials to use for patchwork. Their advantages are that they have a firm weave, are easy to cut, crease and press, and slow to fray. They also come in an astounding range of colours and prints, which means that the choice of palette is endless.

The delicious textures and soft, subtle shades of upholstery/furnishing fabrics do lend themselves to lovely patchworks (see the Beige 4-patch Curtains on pages 115 and 117, and the Brocade and Velvet Throw on page 125), but they are not as easy to handle as lightweight cotton and are best used only for designs with large, simple patch shapes and unpadded items.

Scrap fabrics

In most of my patchwork designs, I like to use as many different fabrics as possible in order to make the colour composition interesting and lively. This makes the designs especially suited to the use of scrap fabrics, leftover pieces big enough for several patches.

If you are already a keen patchwork-quilter, you will already have a collection of scraps that you were just waiting for the perfect opportunity to use up. Once you have chosen the quilt you want to make, my advice would be to start assembling the colours you will need by going through your remnants. Add to this by purchasing small amounts of the missing colours, or even by finding suitable one hundred per cent cotton dresses, blouses or shirts in charity/thrift shops or jumble sales. Remember that polyester and cotton mix fabrics are less desirable for patchwork. Polyester is more difficult to quilt than pure cotton and is crease resistant, which is not an asset for patchwork.

Fabric colours and patterns

Each set of instructions for the patchworks in this book give a 'colour recipe' which is meant to be a guide to choosing fabrics. Read the 'recipe' and study the photograph carefully to decide on your fabric palette.

Most of the designs make use of monochromatic prints or 'tone-on-tone' prints. These prints are composed of one colour in two or more tones, for example a blue monochromatic print would be 'blue-on-blue' – such as a mid and dark blue pattern on a light blue ground or a light blue pattern on a mid blue ground, etc. At a distance small-scale monochromatic prints can appear to be solid colours but have a much more interesting effect than solid-coloured fabrics. The patterns soften and add visual 'texture' to the patchwork geometry.

Many of the designs use prints composed of three or more colours, such as the large-scale floral prints in the Rosy quilts (see pages 18 and 19). Even multi-coloured prints like these usually have a colour that predominates, so pay attention to this hue when selecting them. Alternatively, you can use only the areas of the print that suit your colour scheme, for example by framing the patches over the yellow flowers or only over the magenta flowers in a bold multi-coloured floral.

Aside from prints, stripes and mini-plaids (and sometimes even a few polka dots) can also enliven the patchwork design. In many quilts, using all of these types of fabric patterns together definitely enhances the overall effect. Don't shy away from stripes because you think they may be hard to cut straight or match. There is no need to match stripes in patchwork, and there is no harm in the stripes being slightly off kilter – in fact this can actually be done on purpose for an interesting effect as with the Super Triangles foundation-pieced patches (see page 51).

The only thing to remember when mixing fabrics is that they should all be about the same weight, and if you stick to materials specially made for patchwork this will not be a problem as they are all generally the same lightweight, one hundred per cent cotton.

Fabric quantities

Giving fabric amounts for a patchwork that uses a variety of prints is unfortunately not an exact science, and quantities in instructions should only be considered an approximate guide. It is better to have too much fabric than too little and too many different prints than too few; excess can always be used up in future projects. Some of the instructions in this book give approximate amounts for the patches and others use so many different fabrics that a variety of scraps are recommended.

If you do want to calculate exact fabric amounts for borders, bindings or backings, keep in mind that although specially made patchwork fabrics are usually 44in to 45in (about 112cm) wide, the usable width is only about 42in (107cm) due to slight shrinkage and the necessary removal of selvedges.

Fabric preparation

Always prewash cotton fabric before cutting it into patch shapes. This is a good test for colourfastness and also, if necessary, preshrinks the fabric.

Be sure to wash darks and lights separately. Begin by soaking the fabric in hot soapy water for a few minutes, then look at the water to see if any colour has bled out. To be absolutely sure that the fabric is colourfast, press the wet fabric between white paper towels to check for bleeding.

Rinse the fabric well and when it is still damp, press it with a hot iron. After pressing cut off the selvedges with a rotary cutter (see below for more information about this cutting tool).

Tools and Equipment

Very few tools are needed for patchwork. If you have a sewing workbox, you will probably already have the essentials – fabric scissors, pins, needles, a ruler, tape measure, ironing board and iron. This is all you will need if you are making a simple 'squares' patchwork.

For more complicated patch shapes you will need templates. These can be bought in various sizes or you can make your own (see page 144). For this you will need graph paper, a ruler, a pencil, a pair of paper scissors or a craft knife, and a piece of thin stiff cardboard or specially made template plastic for the template itself.

Probably the most useful patchwork tool to appear this century is the rotary cutter. With a rotary cutter, rotary ruler and rotary cutting board you can cut patches in straight accurate lines in a fraction of the time it takes with scissors.

New gadgets for making patchwork quilts are always coming on the market and you should keep your eye out for anything that you think will save you time and effort.

For machine piecing, of course, you will need a sewing machine. Quilting can also be done on a machine and requires a machine with a 'walking' or darning foot.

The piece of equipment that is invaluable for arranging patches and studying them is a flannel sheet hung or wrapped around a foam-core board from an art supply store or an insulation board from a hardware store. It is possible to arrange a full size patchwork quilt on the floor, but when the floor space just isn't available or if you need to be able to step back far enough to get a full view of the whole thing, a flannel-covered board is just the thing.

And lastly, try to find and purchase a quilter's reducing glass. This helps you to see how a fabric print or even a whole patchwork layout will look at a distance. Reducing glasses are widely available in shops that sell patchwork supplies. Looking through a camera can be an acceptable substitute.

Preparing Patches

Once you have chosen all the fabrics for your quilt, you are ready to start cutting patches. Remember to prepare the fabric lengths and scraps by prewashing, pressing, and cutting off the selvedges first (see above).

The instructions for each quilt in this book include a summary of all the patch shapes used. This will give you a good idea of how complicated or simple a patchwork will be to cut and piece.

Patches for designs made entirely of squares can be cut quickly and accurately with a rotary cutter. Whereas triangle, parallelogram or trapezoid patch shapes will usually require templates for accurate cutting. The easiest patches to cut are those for paper-foundation piecing; they are cut into very rough shapes, stitched to a paper foundation block and then trimmed as the seams are stitched (see pages 146 and 147 for paper foundation piecing).

Rotary cutting

Rotary cutting is especially useful for cutting accurate square patches and for cutting quilt border strips. The rotary mats and transparent acrylic rulers come in a range of sizes. Although it is handy to have a range of large and small mats and rulers, if you want to start out with just one mat and one ruler, chose a 18in by 24in (46cm by 61cm) mat and a 6in by 24in (15cm x 61cm) ruler. With a mat and ruler this size you can cut both border strips and patches with ease. The ruler will have measurement division markings on it as well as 90-, 60- and 45-degree angles.

Before beginning to rotary cut, first press out any creases or fold marks on your fabric. Rotary-cut strips are usually cut across the fabric width from selvedge to selvedge, so you will need to straighten the raw edge. Aligning the selvedges, fold the fabric in half lengthways and smooth it out. Keeping the selvedges together, fold the fabric in half again bringing the selvedges to the fold. On 44in (112cm) wide fabric there will now be an 11in (28cm) long edge to cut strips across.

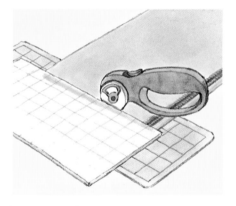

Place the cutting board under the folded fabric and line up the selvedges with a line on the cutting board. Overlap the acrylic rotary ruler about 1/2in (1.5cm) over the raw edge of the fabric, using the lines on the cutting board to make sure that the ruler is perfectly perpendicular to the selvedges. Pressing down on the ruler and the cutter, roll the cutter away from you along the edge of the ruler (see above). Open out the fabric to check the edge. Don't worry if the edge is not *absolutely* straight; a little wiggle won't show once the fabric is stitched in place.

To cut a strip with a rotary cutter, first trim the raw edge of the folded fabric (as shown on the previous page), then align this trimmed edge with the markings on the ruler that match the correct strip width. Cut the strip along the edge of the ruler, keeping the ruler firmly in place and rolling the cutter away from you. Check intermittently to make sure that the raw edge is aligned with the correct position on the ruler.

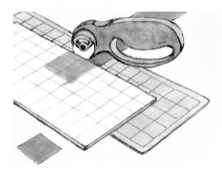

To cut patches, first cut a strip the width of the square, then cut the strip into squares by aligning the ruler markings to the correct measurement (see above). For speed in cutting, stick a piece of masking tape on the wrong side of the ruler along the measurement line that corresponds to the patch size.

With practice you will be able to cut up to six layers of fabric with a large rotary cutter, thereby cutting several patches at once. Just remember to change the cutter blade as soon as it shows the slightest hint of dulling.

Making templates

For patch shapes other than squares and strips, you will need a template of the shape to draw or cut around on to the fabric. Standard-sized templates are available in shops that sell patchwork fabrics and tools. (See page 159 for information on how to obtain Kaffe Fassett *Template Packs*.)

You can also make your own templates. The best material for a template is clear template plastic. Although it is easy to cut, it is very durable and will retain its shape despite being traced around time after time. Its other advantage is its transparency – you can see through it to frame fabric motifs. Thin, stiff cardboard can also be used if template plastic is not available.

To make a template, first trace the actual-sized template shape provided with the quilt instructions either directly on to template plastic, or on to a piece of tracing paper and then on to thin cardboard. Use a ruler for drawing the straight lines, and transfer the cutting line, the seam line and the grain line. Cut out the template.

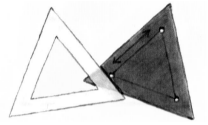

Punch a hole in each corner at each pivot point on the seam line using a ⅛in (3mm) hole punch. This type of template is suitable for machine-pieced patches (see above right). For hand-pieced patches, you should ideally draw the seam line on the fabric and not the cutting line. The seam allowance can then be cut by eye around the patch. You may find that it adds to the accuracy of either machine or hand piecing to draw both the seam line and the cutting line on the fabric. For this you will need to make a window template from template plastic (see above left). A window template is basically just a frame as wide as the seam allowance.

Before going on to cut all your patches, make a patchwork block with test pieces to check the accuracy of your templates. This is especially important with blocks that require inset seams (see page 145).

Cutting template patches

It is a good idea to cut the border strips and binding strips before cutting the patches, and this can be done with a rotary cutter (see page 143 for more on rotary cutters, rotary rulers and rotary cutting mats and detailed instructions for cutting long strips with them).

Next, mark the largest patches on to the fabric. Place the template *face down* on the wrong side of the fabric, aligning the grain line arrow with the straight grain of the fabric (the crossways or the lengthways grain). Press the template down firmly with one hand and draw around it with a sharp pencil in the

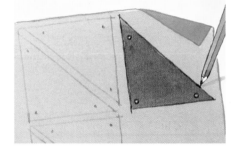

other hand (see above). To save fabric, position the patches as close together as possible or even touching.

You may notice when cutting patches from striped fabrics that although you are drawing around the patches on the straight grain, the outlines do not run exactly with the stripes. Do not worry about this. This will hardly be noticeable once the patches are pieced, and if it is, it just adds to the handmade quality of the patchwork.

Cutting reverse template patches

A reverse template is the mirror image of a patch shape. If the instructions call for a template and the reverse of that template, the same template is used for both shapes.

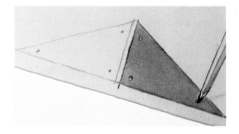

For the reverse of a template, lay the template *face up* on the wrong side of the fabric. Draw around the template in the usual way (see above).

Basic Hand and Machine Piecing

Patches can be joined together by hand or machine. Although machine stitching is much quicker, you might like the idea of being able to carry your patches around with you and work on them in every spare moment. Choose whichever method you find more enjoyable.

Arranging cut patches

Quilt instructions always give a layout for how to arrange the various patch shapes to form the overall geometrical design. It is, of course, possible to just pick your cut patches at random and stitch them together as you pull them out of the pile; but you will achieve a much better effect if you plan your colour arrangement before beginning to piece the patches together.

Lay the patches out on the floor or stick them to a large flannel-covered board, then step back and study the effect. If you don't have access to such a large area, you can arrange individual blocks and, after the blocks have been stitched, arrange the completed blocks on the floor until your are satisfied with the layout.

Creating a stunning colour composition is the most important part of the whole process of patchwork. You will notice that both the colour itself and its value will come into play in your arrangement. The value of a colour is its tone – which ranges from very light tones through to dark. Colours also have relative brightnesses, from dusty and dull to radiant and jewel-like. Dull colours appear greyer than others and tend to recede, while bright, intense colours stand out.

Make sure the colour arrangement is just right before starting to stitch the pieces together. Leave it for a few days and them come back to it and try another arrangement, or try replacing colours that do not seem to work together with new shades. Don't be afraid to position 'mistake' patches inside the arrangement to keep it lively and unpredictable. An unpredictable arrangement will always have more energy and life than one the follows a strict light/dark format.

If the quilt has no border or simply an uncomplicated strip border, it will be easy to change the size of the quilt at this point; but remember to cut any strip borders to the new size.

Machine piecing

If you have a sewing machine, you'll be able to achieve quick results by machine piecing your patches together. Follow the instructions for the order in which to piece the individual patchwork blocks and then assemble the blocks together in rows.

The most important piecing tip for beginners is that you should use the same neutral-coloured thread to piece your entire patchwork. Taupe or light grey thread will work for most patchworks, except when the overall colour scheme is either very dark or very light. For a very dark design, use charcoal thread and for a very light, ecru. Be sure to purchase one hundred per cent cotton thread.

Pin the patches together, right sides facing and matching the seam lines and corner points carefully. (You may find that you can stitch small squares together without pinning, so try both ways.) Then machine stitch, using the correct seam allowance and removing each pin before the needle reaches it. Except for inset seams (see below), machine stitched patchwork seams are sewn from raw edge to raw edge. (There is no need to work backstitches at the beginning and end of each patch, since the stitches will be secured by crossing seam lines as the pieces are joined together.)

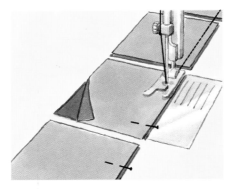

You can save both time and thread by chain piecing. This is done by feeding through the pinned together patches one after another without lifting the presser foot. Let the machine stitch in the air a few times before it reaches the next pair of patches (see above).

Pressing patch seams

After each seam has been stitched, press the seams flat to imbed the stitches. Then, if the patches have been chain-pieced, cut them apart. Next, open out the patches and press the seam allowances to one side.

Continue joining the patches into blocks, then the blocks into rows as directed, pressing all the seam allowances

in one row in the same direction. After all the blocks are joined into rows, join the rows together. Try to press the seam allowances in every other row in the opposite direction so that you don't have to stitch through two layers of seam allowances when joining the rows.

Hand piecing blocks

Hand stitching your patches together is time-consuming, but it does give a beautiful handmade finish to the patchwork. Just lay a hand-stitched and a machine-stitched block side by side and the striking difference in the overall look will be obvious.

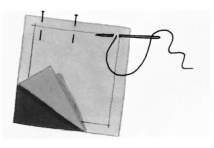

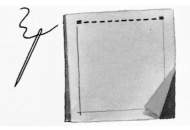

To hand piece two patches, pin them right sides together so that the pencilled seam lines are facing outwards. Using a single strand of thread, secure the end with a couple of backstitches (see above top). Then work short, even running stitches along the seam line, beginning and ending at the seam-line corners (see above). When hand piecing, never stitch across the seam allowances.

Press the seam allowances to one side as for machine-pieced seams, or press all seam allowances open.

Stitching inset seams

You will find that most patches can be joined together with a straight seam line, but with some patchwork layouts a patch will need to be sewn into a corner formed by two other patches. This will require a seam line that turns a corner – called an inset seam.

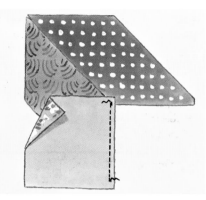

First, align the patches along one side of the angle and pin, matching up the corner points exactly. Machine stitch along the seam line of this edge up to the corner point and work a few backstitches to secure (see above).

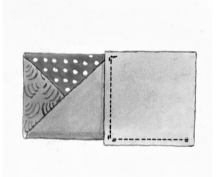

Then pivot the set-in patch, align the adjacent side with the edge of the next patch and pin. Beginning exactly at the corner point, work a few backstitches to secure, then machine stitch along the seam line to the outer edge of the patches (see above).

Trim away excess fabric from the seam allowance at the corner of the inset patch as necessary. Press the new seams, easing the corner into the correct shape (see above).

Paper Foundation Piecing

In paper foundation piecing the patchwork block design is drawn on a piece of paper the exact size of the block. Each patch shape on the paper is numbered to indicate the sequence in which the patches should be stitched. During the stitching process, the patches are joined together under the paper foundation piece with the patch seams piercing the fabric layers and the paper.

This techniques has many advantages. It requires little skill and is very accurate. It is also incredibly quick because there is no need for cutting patches with templates; all the fabric pieces are cut in very rough shapes and trimmed as they are stitched to the paper foundation.

Another advantage of paper foundation piecing is that it allows you to use patches that are not cut on the straight grain of the fabric. The paper provides the stability needed to keep the off-grain seams from stretching. Not having to pay attention to cutting exactly on the grain line speeds up the piecing process considerably. It also enables you to design patchworks with stripes, plaids and prints set at random angles (see instructions for the Super Triangles Baby Quilt on pages 50–55).

Preparing paper foundations

You will need a paper foundation for each of the blocks being made with the technique. Either photocopy the diagram of the foundation piece or draw it on graph paper. If you are drawing the design, be as accurate as possible.

Always use a 'first generation' photocopy or the drawing as the master for the block design and take all of the photocopies of it directly from this master. Try to avoid making photocopies of photocopies, since the design will become distorted. The number of copies required will be given in the quilt instructions.

Cut out each paper foundation along the outer cutting line, which includes the seam allowance. If there are blocks of different sizes in the patchwork, check the master foundation pieces to make sure that they are all the correct size to fit together accurately.

Cutting fabric pieces

Before beginning to stitch the block, cut the fabric pieces for each of the numbered areas on the foundation piece. The size and shape of the fabric pieces need only be approximate. Allow for about a 1/2in (12mm) seam allowance, and if in doubt, cut the piece bigger rather than smaller.

The numbered side of the foundation paper is the wrong side of the block, so cut the fabric pieces with the wrong side facing up.

Stitching the blocks

Once the fabric pieces are ready, insert a 90/14 machine needle. Then set the sewing machine stitch length to a short stitch – about 18 to 20 stitches per inch (2.5cm). The large needle and short stitch will help to perforate the paper, making it easier to tear away later.

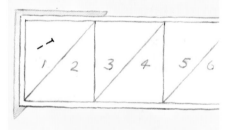

Take the fabric piece for area no. 1 and pin it to the back of the foundation paper under area no. 1 of the block, with the wrong side of the fabric facing the unmarked side of the paper (see above). Hold the paper up to the light to make sure that the fabric piece covers the area and extends at least 1/4in (6mm) beyond the stitching lines.

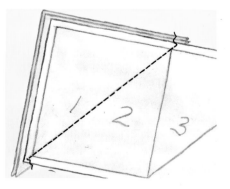

Next, place piece no. 2 on top of no. 1 (see above) with the right sides facing and the raw edges aligned along the seam-line edge. Holding the patches in place, machine stitch along the seam line between no. 1 and no. 2 with the marked side of the paper block facing upwards. Begin and end the stitching in the seam allowance so that it extends slightly beyond each end of the seam line as shown. The ends of the stitching will be secured by future seams.

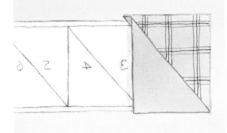

Trim the seam allowance to ¼in (6mm) using a small, sharp pair of scissors. Then open out piece no. 2 (see above), finger press the seam and press with a hot iron but no steam; for small pieces, only finger-pressing the seam will be adequate. Continue adding pieces in this way, joining them in the sequence marked on the block.

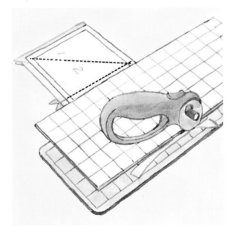

After the last patch has been stitched in place on the foundation paper, trim away the excess fabric around the edge of the block with a rotary cutter and ruler, leaving the designated seam allowance around the outer edge of the finished block (see above).

Leave the paper foundation piece on the block until all the blocks have been stitched together, but tear out any paper corners that will make the seams too bulky. Note that the right side of the finished block is the reverse image of

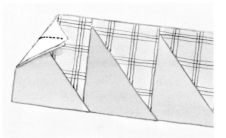

the marked side of the foundation paper (see above). Once all the blocks are joined, tear away all of the paper.

Quilting and Finishing

After you have finished piecing your patchwork, press it carefully. It is now ready to be quilted if quilting is required. However, many items of patchwork, such as cushion covers, throws, curtains and table covers need only be backed.

Quilting patterns

Patchwork quilting is the stitching that joins together the three layers of the quilt sandwich – top, batting/wadding and backing. For patchworks that have a strong design story of their own, try to chose a quilting pattern that does not detract from the patchwork. In some instances you will find that stitch-in-the-ditch quilting is the perfect choice, since the quilting lines are stitched into the patch seam lines making the quilting stitches invisible on the right side of the patchwork.

Outline quilting is another simple quilting pattern that will suit many patchwork designs. It is worked by stitching ¼in (6mm) from the patch seam lines.

You will need to mark more complicated quilting patterns on the right side of the piece patchwork before the quilt layers are joined. The marking can be done with specially designed quilting markers. If you are in doubt about which quilting pattern to chose, test the pattern on a spare pieced block. This will also be a good way to check whether your chosen quilting thread is a suitable colour.

Quilting thread is a specially made cotton thread that is thicker and stronger than ordinary sewing thread. The thread colour should usually blend

invisibly into the overall colour of the patchwork quilt when it is viewed from a distance.

Using a quilting stencil is the easiest way to mark a complicated pattern on to the fabric. These stencils are widely available in shops that sell patchwork and quilting materials.

Preparing the backing and batting

Cut the selvedges off of the backing fabric, then seam the pieces together to form a backing at least 3 inches (7.5cm) bigger all around than the patchwork. It is best to join the pieces so that the seam lines run lengthways.

If the batting/wadding has been rolled, unroll it and let it rest before cutting it to about the same size as the backing. Batting comes in various thicknesses, but a pure cotton or mixed cotton and polyester batting which is fairly thin, will be a good choice for most quilts. Thicker batting is usually only suitable when the quilt layers are being tied together. A hundred per cent cotton batting will give your quilt the attractive, relatively flat appearance of an antique quilt.

Basting the quilt layers

Lay out the backing wrong side up and smooth it out. Place the batting on top of the backing, then lay the pieced patchwork right side up on top of the batting and smooth it out.

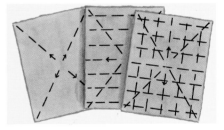

Beginning at the centre, baste two diagonal lines from corner to corner through the layers (see above left). Make stitches about 3 inches (7.5cm) long and try not to lift the layers too much as you stitch. Then, again always beginning at the centre and working outwards, baste horizontal and vertical lines across the layers (see above centre and right). The basting lines should be about 4 inches (10cm) apart.

Hand Quilting

Hand quilting is best done with the quilt layers mounted in a quilting frame or hoop. Thread a short quilting needle (an 8 to 11 between) with an 18in (46cm) length of special cotton quilting thread and knot the end. With the quilt top facing upwards and beginning at the centre of the basted quilt layers, insert the needle through the top about ½in (12mm) from the starting point and into the batting, then bring it out at the starting point. Pull the thread to pop the knot into the batting.

Loading about three or four stitches on to the needle and working with one hand under the quilt to help the needle back up again, make short, even running stitches. Pull the thread through and continue along the quilting line in this way.

It is more important to make even stitches on both sides of the quilt than to make small ones. When the thread is about to run out, make a small backstitch, then pierce this backstitch to anchor it and run the thread end through into the batting.

Machine quilting

For machine quilting, use a walking foot for straight lines and a darning foot for curved lines. Use regular sewing thread and choose a colour that blends with the overall colour of the patchwork for the top thread and one that matches the backing for the bobbin thread. Begin and end the quilting lines with very short stitches to secure, leaving long ends to thread into the batting later. Follow the machine manual for tips on using the walking or darning feet.

Tying quilts

If you don't have the time needed for allover quilting, you can tie together the basted layers of your patchwork quilt. Make sure that you are using a batting with a high loft, because thin cotton battings usually require quite close quilting lines.

Use a sharp needle with a large eye and wool yarn, thick embroidery thread or narrow ribbon for the tying. For simple tying, cut a 7in (18cm) length of yarn and thread the needle.

Beginning the tying at the centre of the quilt, make a small stitch through all three layers (see fig 17, above left). Tie the two ends of the yarn into a double knot (see fig 17, above right) and trim. If you are making bows, use a longer length of thread.

Binding quilt edges

Once the quilt has been quilted or tied together, remove the basting threads. Then baste around the quilt just under ¼in (about 5mm) from the edge of the patchwork. Trim the outer edge of the quilt, cutting away the excess batting and backing right up to the edge of the patchwork and, if necessary, straightening the edge of the patchwork in the process.

Cut 2in (5cm) wide binding strips either on the straight grain or on the bias. (Striped fabrics look especially effective when cut on the bias to form diagonal stripes around the edge of the patchwork.) Join these binding strips end-to-end with diagonal seams until the strip is long enough to fit around the edge.

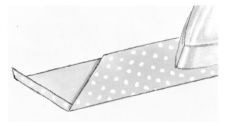

Cut the beginning end of the binding strip at a 45 degree angle, turn ¼in (6mm) to the wrong side along this cut end, and press. Then fold the strip in half lengthways with the wrong sides together and press (see above).

Place the doubled binding on the right side of the quilt, with the longer side facing the quilt and aligning the raw edges. Stitch from the second folded edge on the binding ¼in (6mm) from the edge up to ¼in (6mm) from the first

corner (see above). Make a few backstitches and cut the thread ends.

Fold the binding up, making a 45 degree angle (see above left). Keeping the diagonal fold in place, fold the binding back down and align the edge with the next side of the quilt. Beginning at the point where the last stitching ended, stitch down the next side (see above right).

Continue stitching the binding in place all around the edge in this way, tucking the end inside the beginning of the binding (see above).

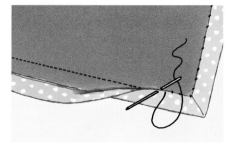

Turn the folded edge of the binding to the back. Hand stitch in place, folding a mitre at each corner (see above).

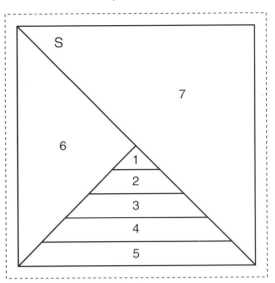

Templates

The templates and foundation pieces for the patchworks are given on pages 149 through 158. The templates are all shown actual size. The foundation pieces have been reduced to 50 per cent; for the correct size, redraw these blocks on graph paper to twice as large or enlarge 200 per cent on a photocopier.

The seam lines on the templates and the foundation pieces are indicated by solid lines and the cutting lines by broken lines.

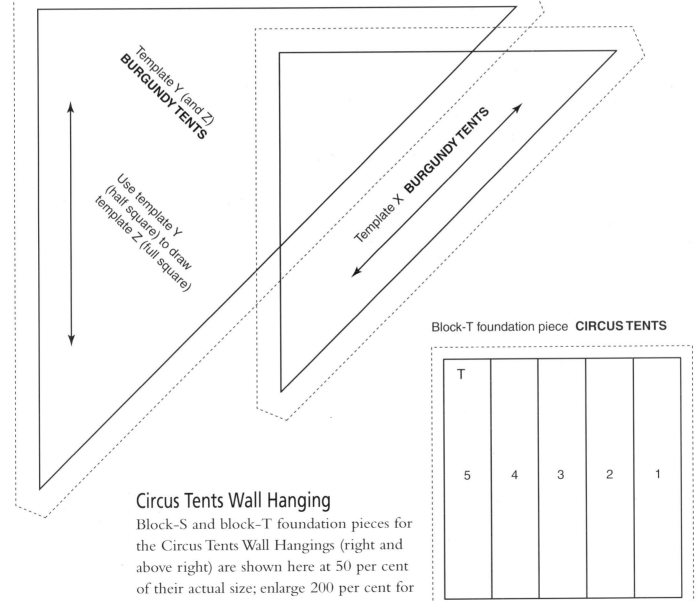

Template Y (and Z) **BURGUNDY TENTS**

Use template Y (half square) to draw template Z (full square)

Template X **BURGUNDY TENTS**

Block-T foundation piece **CIRCUS TENTS**

Circus Tents Wall Hanging

Block-S and block-T foundation pieces for the Circus Tents Wall Hangings (right and above right) are shown here at 50 per cent of their actual size; enlarge 200 per cent for the correct size.

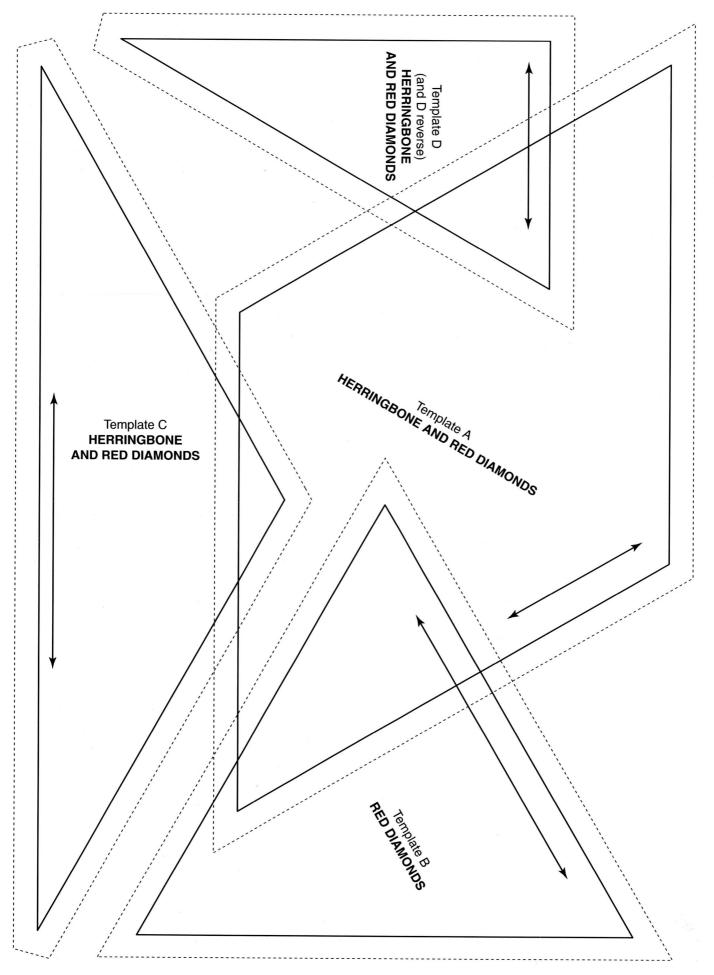

Template D
(and D reverse)
**HERRINGBONE
AND RED DIAMONDS**

Template A
HERRINGBONE AND RED DIAMONDS

Template C
**HERRINGBONE
AND RED DIAMONDS**

Template B
RED DIAMONDS

150

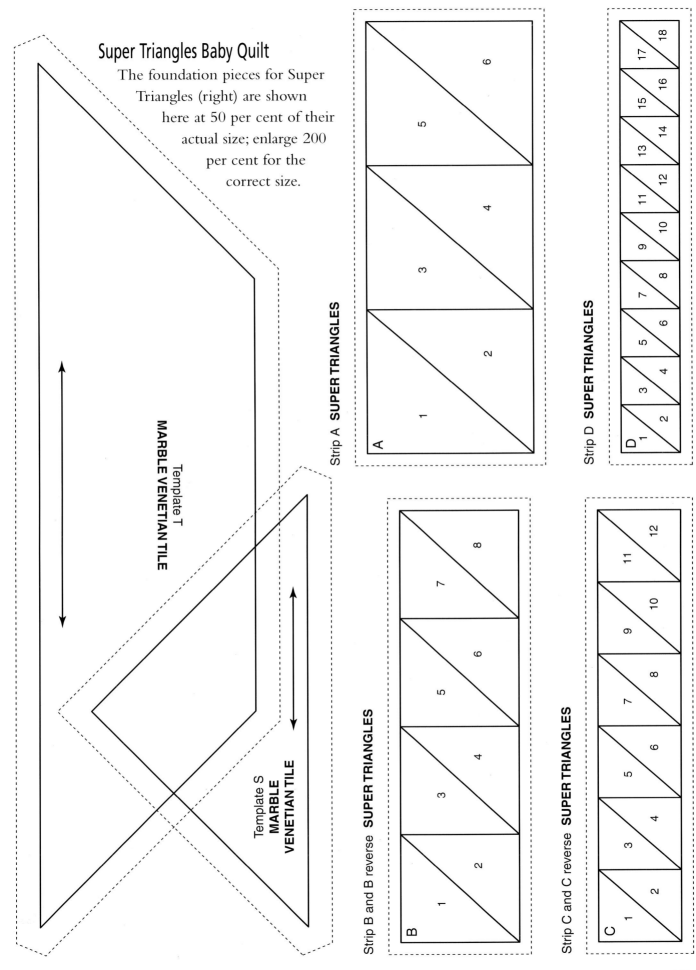

Super Triangles Baby Quilt

The foundation pieces for Super Triangles (right) are shown here at 50 per cent of their actual size; enlarge 200 per cent for the correct size.

Template T
MARBLE VENETIAN TILE

Template S
**MARBLE
VENETIAN TILE**

Strip A **SUPER TRIANGLES**

A

Strip D **SUPER TRIANGLES**

D

Strip B and B reverse **SUPER TRIANGLES**

B

Strip C and C reverse **SUPER TRIANGLES**

C

Block-S (and S-reverse) foundation piece PENNANTS

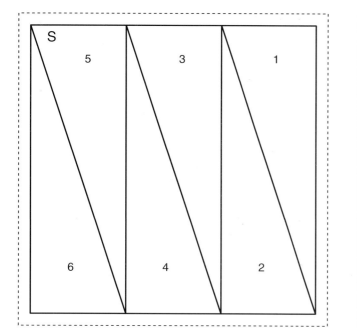

Block-T (and T-reverse) foundation piece PENNANTS

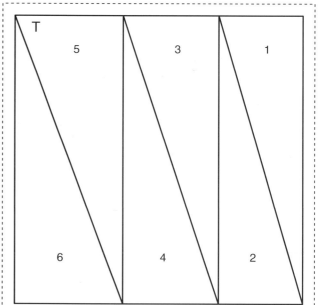

Pennants

Blocks S, S-reverse, T and T-reverse and strips U and V for the Pennants quilts (above and facing page) are shown here at 50 per cent of their actual size; enlarge 200 per cent for the correct size.

Template X **PENNANTS**

Template Y (and Y reverse) **PENNANTS**

Strip-U foundation piece **PENNANTS**

U

5

6

3

4

1

2

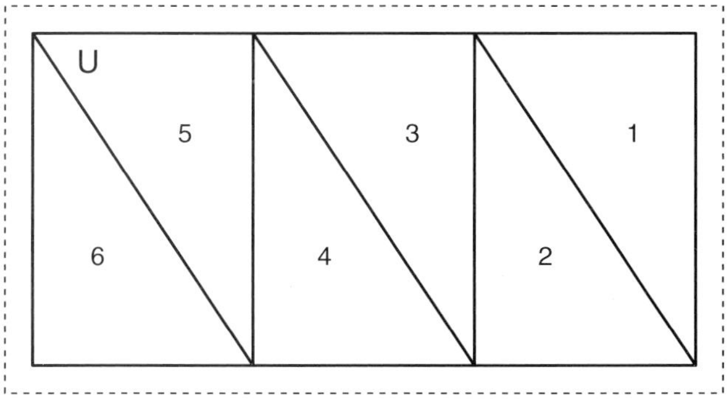

Strip-V foundation piece **PENNANTS**

V

5

6

3

4

1

2

Template V
TAUPE LATTICE

Template S
TAUPE LATTICE

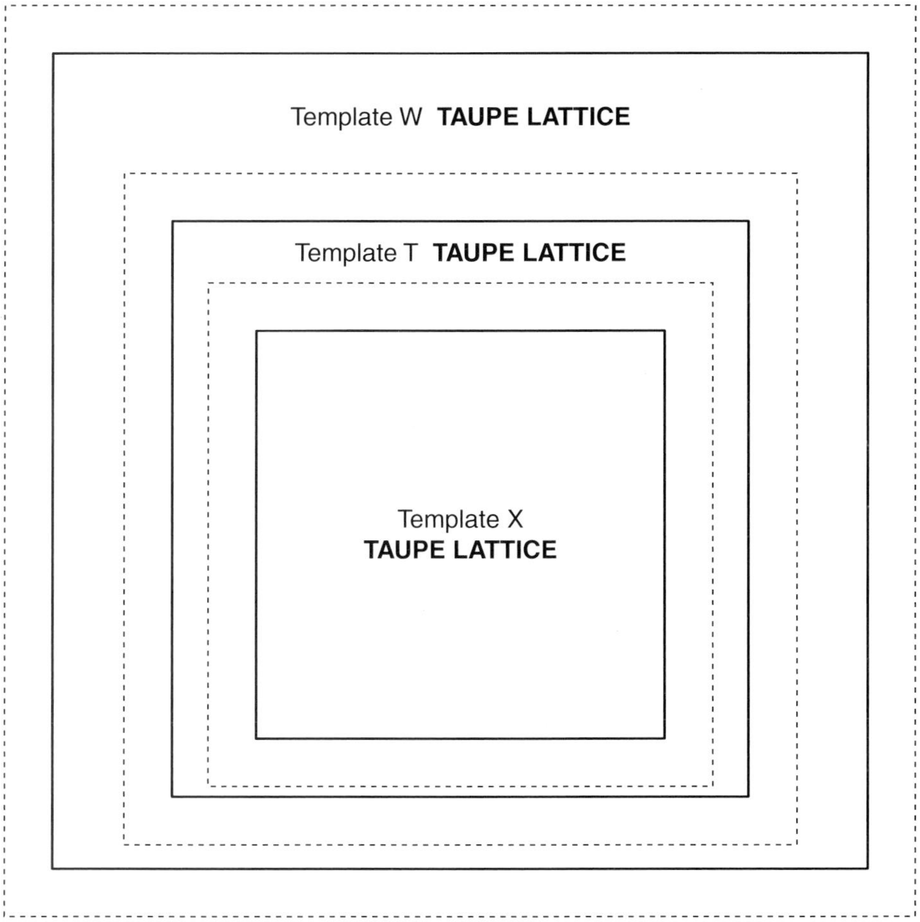

Template W **TAUPE LATTICE**

Template T **TAUPE LATTICE**

Template X
TAUPE LATTICE

Template U
TAUPE LATTICE

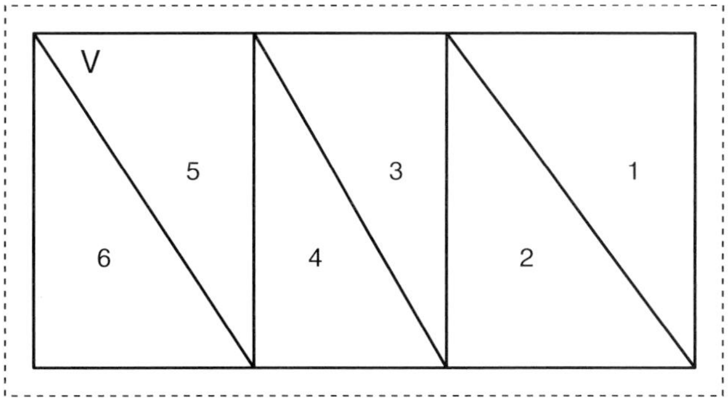

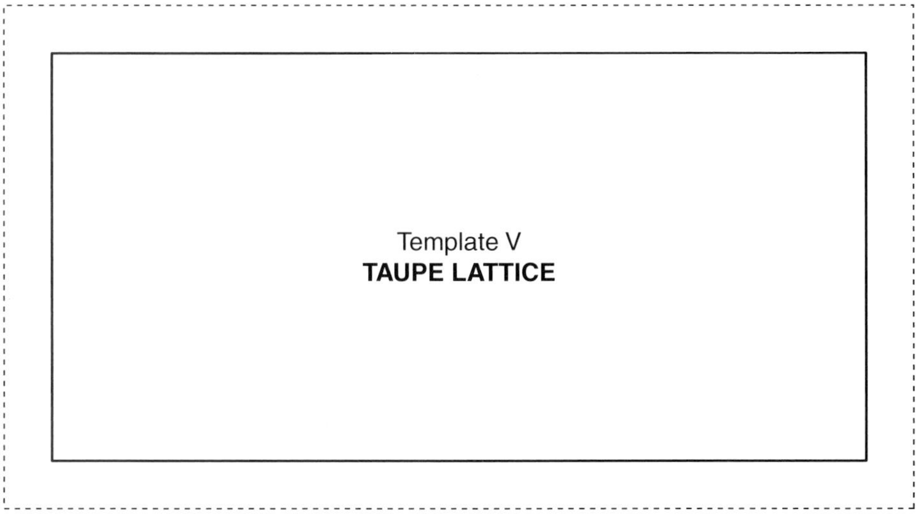

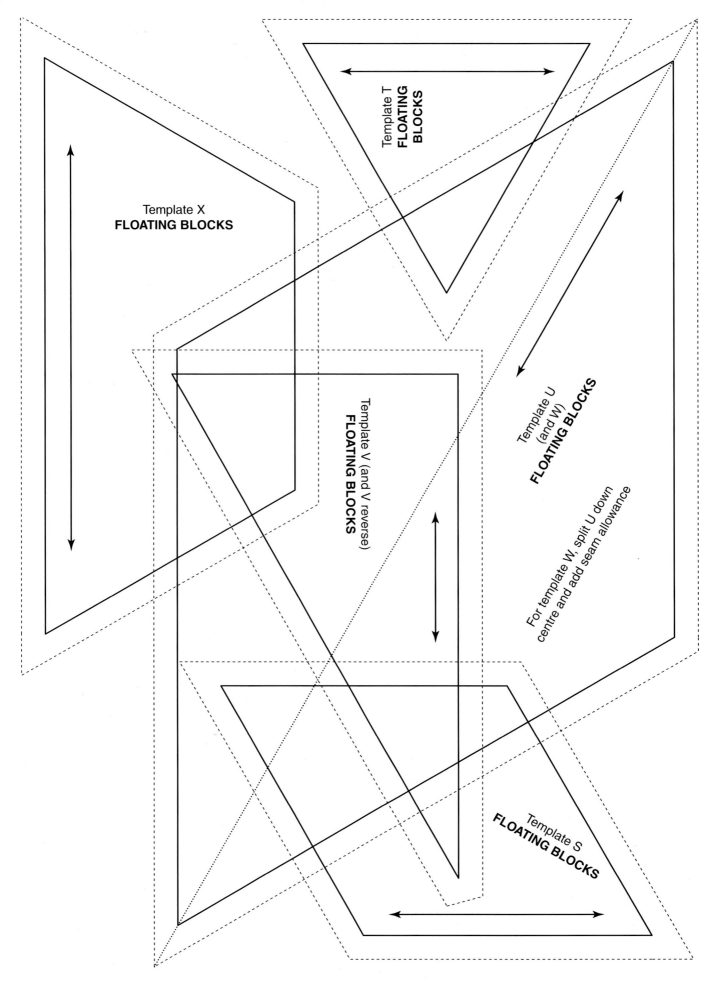

Template T
FLOATING BLOCKS

Template X
FLOATING BLOCKS

Template V (and V reverse)
FLOATING BLOCKS

Template U
(and W)
FLOATING BLOCKS

For template W, split U down
centre and add seam allowance

Template S
FLOATING BLOCKS

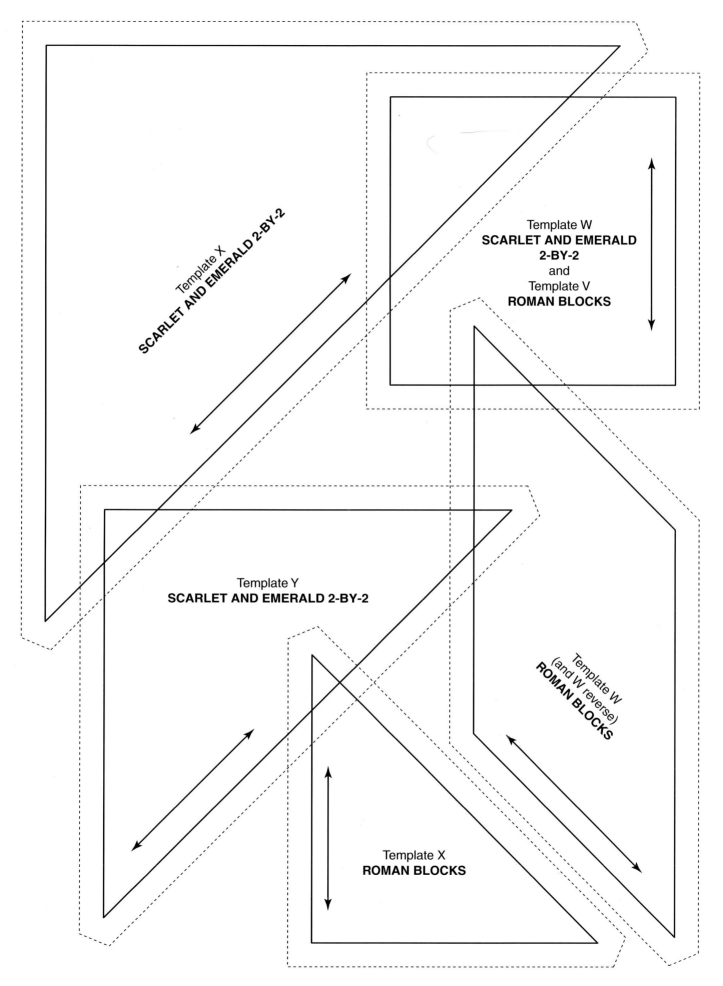

Template X
SCARLET AND EMERALD 2-BY-2

Template W
**SCARLET AND EMERALD
2-BY-2**
and
Template V
ROMAN BLOCKS

Template Y
SCARLET AND EMERALD 2-BY-2

Template W
(and W reverse)
ROMAN BLOCKS

Template X
ROMAN BLOCKS

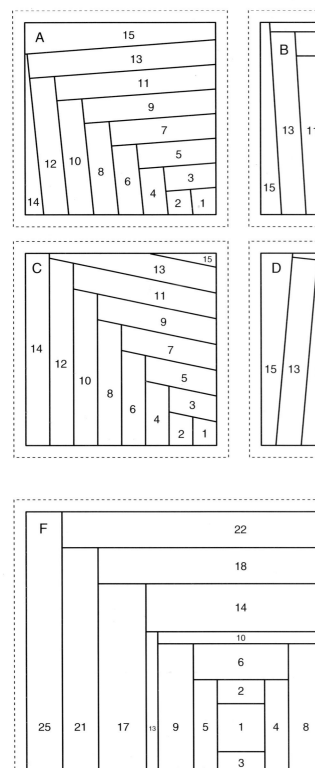

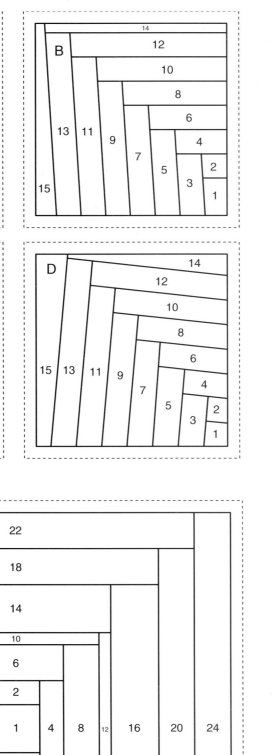

Crazy Squares Cushion and Table Runner

Block A, B, C and D foundation pieces for the Crazy Squares cushion and table runner (left) are shown here at 50 per cent of their actual size; enlarge 200 per cent for the correct size.

Jewel Squares Window Blind

Block A, B, C, D, E and F foundation pieces for the Jewel Squares Window Blind (below and below left and on pages 157 and 158) are shown here at 50 per cent of their actual size; enlarge 200 per cent for the correct size.

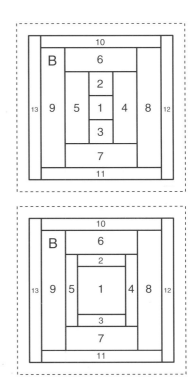

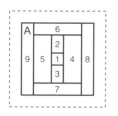

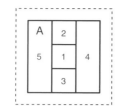

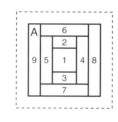

Jewel Squares Window Blind

See page 156 for information about these foundation pieces.

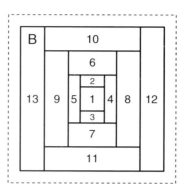

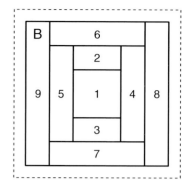

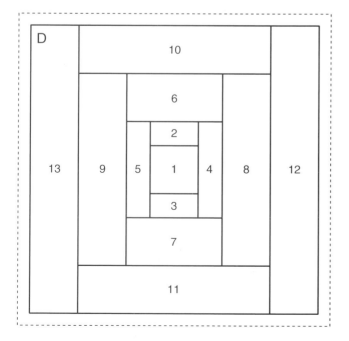

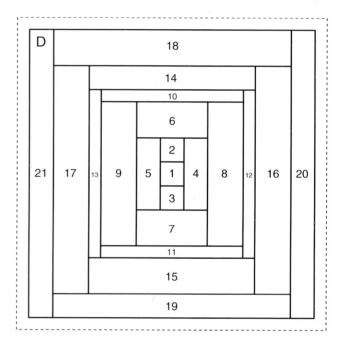

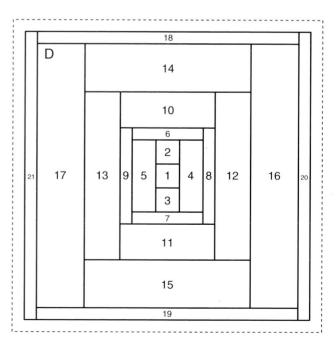

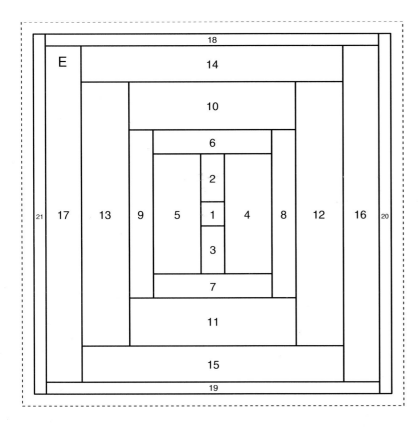

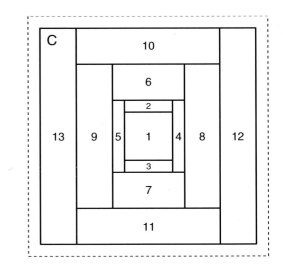

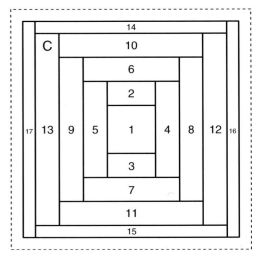

Jewel Squares Window Blind

See page 156 for information about these foundation pieces.

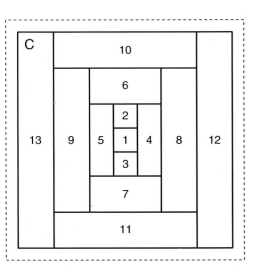

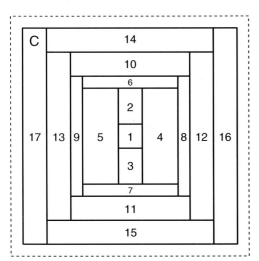

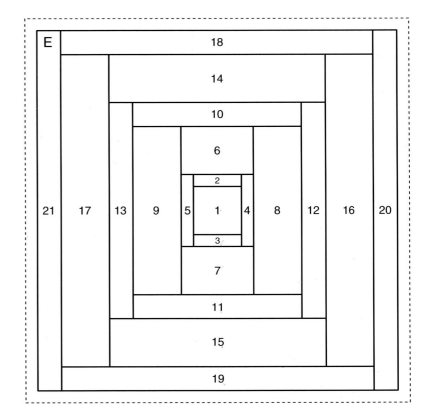

KAFFE FASSETT PATCHWORK KITS

The following Kaffe Fassett patchworks are available as kits. The kits contain fabrics chosen by Kaffe to create the look and feel of the original patchworks featured in this book, full instructions and, where necessary, foundation pieces and/or templates. For those who want to select their own fabrics, there are packs of templates and/or foundation pieces available separately for some of the designs as indicated below:

pages 14 and 15 Pinafore-print Diamonds Kit – also Template Pack; *page 16* Pale Floating Blocks – Template Pack only; *page 26* Herringbone Baby Kit – also Template Pack; *page 31* Frothy Kit – also Template Pack; *pages 2 and 37* Citrus and Delft 2-by-2 Kit; *page 37* Blue Roman Blocks – Template Pack only; *page 39* Yellow Pennants – also Foundation-piece/Template Pack; *page 41* Pink and Blue Pennants Kit – also Foundation-piece/Template Pack; *page 46* Yellow Stripes Cushion Kit; *page 46* Venetian Tile Cushion Kit – also Template Pack; *page 48* Crazy Squares – Foundation-piece Pack only; *page 51* Super Triangles Baby – Foundation-piece Pack only; *page 57* Circus Tents – Foundation-piece Pack only; *page 79* Red Diamonds Kit – also Template Pack; *page 93* Navy Bricks Kit; *page 94* Tweed Floating Blocks – Template Pack only; *page 101* Pink Roman Blocks – Template Pack only; *page 111* Marble Venetian Tile Kit – also Template Pack; *page 120* Striped Diamonds Kit – also Template Pack; *page 120* Jewel Floating Blocks Kit – also Template Pack; *page 121* Striped Venetian Tile Kit – also Template Pack; *page 123* Burgundy Tents Kit – also Template Pack; *page 139* Jewel Squares Kit – also Foundation-piece Pack.

PATCHWORK KIT SUPPLIERS

For information on how to obtain Kaffe Fassett patchwork kits, and template and foundation-piece packs, contact one of the following:
WESTMINSTER FIBERS, 5 Northern Boulevard, Amherst, NH 03031, U.S.A. Tel: (603) 886 5041. Fax: (603) 886 1056.
ROWAN, Green Lane Mill, Washpit, Holmfirth, Huddersfield HD7 1RW, West Yorkshire, U.K. Tel: (01484) 681 881. Fax: (01484) 687 920.
KAFFE FASSETT DESIGNS LTD, 3 Saville Row, Bath BA1 2QP, U.K. Tel: (01225) 484 215. Fax: (01225) 484 216.
See also Supplier's Credits (right).

KAFFE FASSETT NEEDLEPOINT KITS

The following Kaffe Fassett needlepoint cushions are featured in the book and are available as kits from EHRMAN TAPESTRY:
page 10 Patchwork Rose; *page 11* Roman Blocks; *page 41* Sunset Sails by Brandon Mably for the Kaffe Fassett Design Studio; *page 67* California Grapes, Ribbon and Rose; *page 115* Waterlily; *page 122* Ribbon Nosegay. These designs can be seen stitched up in the EHRMAN shop in Kensington Church Street in London (see address below). The shop

stocks the full range of Kaffe Fassett designs. To order kits, contact one of the following:
U.K.: EHRMAN (shop), 14-16 Lancer Square, Kensington Church Street, London W8 4EP, England. Shop tel: (0171) 937 8123. Telephone ordering: (0181) 573 4891. Fax: (0171) 937 8552.
U.S.A.: EHRMAN TAPESTRY, 5300 Dorsey Hall Drive, Suite 110, Ellicott City, Maryland 21042. Tel: toll free order line (888) 826 8600, customer service (410) 884 7944. Fax: (410) 884 0598. E-mail: usehrman@mail.clark.net
Canada: POINTERS, 99 Yorkville Avenue, Unit 103, Toronto, Ontario MRR 3K5. Tel: (416) 962 9998 or 1 (800) 465 5290. Fax: (416)962 6889.
Australia: TAPESTRY ROSE, PO Box 366, Canterbury 3126. Tel: (03) 9804 0606.
New Zealand: QUALITY HANDCRAFTS, PO Box 1486, Auckland. Tel: (09) 411 8645.
South Africa: SPEAKERS INTERNATIONAL, Box 92043, Norwood 2117. Tel: (0027) 11 640 6722.

SUPPLIERS' CREDITS

The author and publisher would like to thank the following suppliers in the U.S.A. for the fabrics and other materials. (Note that the shops with an asterisk ★ offer mail order service for Kaffe Fassett patchwork kits, template and foundation-piece packs, and Stripe Fabrics.)
Upholstery/furnishing fabrics:
ABC CARPET AND HOME, 888 Broadway, New York, NY 10003. Tel: (212) 473 3000.
Hand-blocked fabrics:
CHARME RUSTIQUE, 3 Claremont Road, Bernardsville, NJ 07924. Tel: (908) 221 1088.
Patchwork fabrics, batting and notions:
★THE COUNTRY QUILT SHOP, 515 Stump Road, Montgomeryville, PA 18936. Tel: (215) 855 5554 or (888) 627 6969. E-mail: http://iypn.com/cqs
SEW SMART, 53 W State Street, Doylestown, PA 18901. Tel: (215) 345 7990.
★STRAW INTO GOLD, 3006 San Pablo Avenue, Berkeley, CA 94702. Tel: (510) 548 5243. Fax: (510) 548 3453. E-mail: http://www.straw.com/sig
★THE SUMMER HOUSE, 6375 Oley Turnpike Road, Oley, PA 19547. Tel: (610) 689 9090. Fax: (610) 689 4713. E-mail: summerh@dca.net
WEST END FABRIC, 588 River Road, Fair Haven, NJ 07704. Tel: (908) 747 4838.
G STREET FABRICS, 11854 Rockville Pike, Rockville, MD 20852. Tel: (301) 231 8998.
Bernina sewing machine sales and service:
BYRNE SEWING CONNECTION, 86 W State Street, Doylestown,PA 18901. Tel: (215) 230 9411.

PHOTO CREDITS

All of the project photographs in the book and the back cover were shot by Debbie Patterson. The patchwork flat shots, including the front cover shot, were taken by Dave King. The publishers would like to thank the following for the remaining photography. *8 top, 90 top right, 93, 111 and 120 left,*

Irving Schild; *11 top right, 12 bottom right and 34 top right,* Steve Lovi; *34 top left and 118 top left,* Bridgeman Art Library; *64 top left and bottom right,* The Metropolitan Museum of Art, Purchase, Bequest of Charles Allen Munn by exchange, Fosburgh Fund, Inc and Mr and Mrs J William Middendorf II Gifts and Hentry G Keasbey Bequest, 1967 (67.111); *90 bottom left,* André Bruyère.

ACKNOWLEDGMENTS

Making the quilts was a humongous task miraculously achieved in under two years. Kaffe and Liza would like to thank the following whose willing help made this possible—
Susan Maynard Arnold, Susan R Dague, Mary Evans, Meg Maas, Bobbi Penniman, Patricia W Petrie, Evelyn Portrait, Anne M Soriero and Janet E Stoner pieced the glorious patchworks; Bobbi Penniman and Pat Burns stitched the glorious quilting; Martha T Brown, Yvonne Mably, Joanne M Raab, Nana Sparrow and Cheryl Smith made the glorious finishing touches; Cyndi Hershey, Joy Bohanan, Sandy Muckenthaler at HOFFMAN CALIFORNIA, Colette de Marco, Thana Attieh, Liz H Muchmore, Jill Krasner, Evan Cole, the HOBBS BONDED FIBER CO and BERNINA OF AMERICA facilitated the search for fabric, notions, batting and other necessities; Irving Schild and John Vullierme, the cast and crew of CBS's Sunday Morning, Jane Zell Rawes and the Hazmats Quilting Guild made the photo shoot in the U.S.A. an enjoyable event; Holly Fassett, Susan Druding, June and Kenneth Bridgewater, Stephen Sheard, Louisa Harding, Simon Cockin and Judy Roche gave their help generously; and Sigmund Roos and Richard Womersley offered much appreciated advice and moral support.

Once made, these quilts needed surroundings that set off their complex mixtures of fabrics. Very special gratitude goes to Sue Godley, Anne Marie and Don Evans, June Henry, The American Museum in Bath, C R Upton's pumpkin farm in Sussex, Judith E Melson, and David April and Mary Bluder at Fonthill in Doylestown, Pennsylvania for supplying unique interiors and exteriors. Thanks to Scumble Goosie in Stroud for the loan of furniture and to Peter Adler for the loan of his antique quilt. For wallpapers, huge thanks to Tricia Guild of Designers Guild, Alexander Beauchamp (Wallpapers and Fabrics Ltd) and Sandersons.

Thanks to Steve Lovi for extra photos and his critical eye.

Special thanks to Sally Harding, Polly Dawes, Denise Bates and Debbie Patterson for their endless and inspiring work on this book, and big thanks to Drew, Alexandra and Elizabeth Lucy, Paula and William Roos, Nancy and Charles Lucy, and Joel Fram for their inspiration, help, nourishment and encouragement.

And once again a round of applause to Brandon Mably for running the whole circus and keeping us all fed at the same time.

Index

Page numbers in *italic* refer to main illustrations